Victor Lundy Artist Architect

Victor Lundy Artist Architect

Donna Kacmar, editor

Princeton Architectural Press · New York

Published by
Princeton Architectural Press
A McEvoy Group company
202 Warren Street, Hudson, NY 12534
Visit our website at www.papress.com

Princeton Architectural Press is a leading publisher in architecture,
design, photography, landscape, and visual culture. We create
fine books and stationery of unsurpassed quality and production values.
With more than one thousand titles published, we find design
everywhere and in the most unlikely places.

Editor: Kristen Hewitt
Designer: Anjali Pala, Miko McGinty Inc.

Front cover:
I. Miller Showroom, Grand Hall, New York City, 1962
Photograph by George Cserna. Avery Architectural & Fine Arts Library,
Columbia University

Special thanks to: Paula Baver, Janet Behning, Nolan Boomer,
Abby Bussel, Benjamin English, Jan Cigliano Hartman, Susan Hershberg,
Kristen Hewitt, Lia Hunt, Valerie Kamen, Sara McKay, Eliana Miller, Nina Pick,
Wes Seeley, Rob Shaeffer, Sara Stemen, Marisa Tesoro, Paul Wagner,
and Joseph Weston of Princeton Architectural Press
—Kevin C. Lippert, publisher

Library of Congress Cataloging-in-Publication Data
Names: Kacmar, Donna, editor. | Tehrani, Nader, 1963– writer of foreword.
Title: Victor Lundy : artist architect / edited by Donna Kacmar.
Other titles: Victor Lundy (Princeton Architectural Press)
Description: First edition. | New York : Princeton Architectural Press, 2018.
 | Includes bibliographical references.
Identifiers: LCCN 2017060832 | ISBN 9781616896614 (hardcover : alk. paper)
Subjects: LCSH: Lundy, Victor Alfred, 1923– | Midcentury modern
 (Architecture)--United States.
Classification: LCC NA737.L87 V53 2018 | DDC 720.92--dc23
LC record available at https://lccn.loc.gov/2017060832

Contents

Foreword

Nader Tehrani

Of the many notable modernists who led productive practices while undertaking extraordinary experimentation, there is no one like Victor Lundy. I was fortunate to be paired with Lundy for the *Beyond the Harvard Box* symposium, a 2006 event that assembled some of the key architectural protagonists of the postwar era to discuss the contemporary significance of the much-maligned modern "box," seen by many as brutalist or lacking in craft. Though Lundy shared temporal and institutional associations with many of his peers, his work differed significantly—in great part due to his detailed material explorations and the risks he took with building forms; at once sculptural and semantically loaded, his work displays qualities that evaded the compositional and tactical conventions of the time.

Much like other figures who do not fit easily within the canon of modern architecture, such as Togo Murano in Japan or Luigi Caccia Dominioni in Italy, Lundy's work escapes easy categorization. With a broad adaptability to varied building types and materials, he has never relied on a single aesthetic to establish his authorship. This aspect of Lundy's work renders it not only emblematic of its time but also timeless, as evidenced in its many alignments with methodological, ideological, and technological affinities of contemporary architecture.

In preparation for our public dialogue, I had the opportunity to meet with Lundy and gain a better understanding of the ways in which, I believe, his work avoids some of the more complacent aspects of the modern experiment. The majority of his projects are driven from the bottom up, with intensive material experimentation at the scale of the detail.

The subsequent aggregation, assembly, and composition of those details commonly produces the spatial and formal inventions that are characteristic of his work. This emphasis on material behavior, units of construction, and the assembly process prioritizes the operational nature of design protocols over a focus on the end product alone, and it's one of the reasons that no two Lundy projects look alike.

Though trained in both Beaux-Arts and modernist pedagogies, in which designs emerged top-down with a parti or diagram guiding the process, Lundy has a protean ability to work concurrently through multiple scales, which gives his work a critical edge. Today, he stands out for his persistent attention to material agency: the careful engagement of material technologies as the prerequisite to design. What his work demonstrates is the possibility that rules of composition do not necessarily need to preempt design approaches. For this reason, even though many of Lundy's buildings manifest well-known formal and figural strategies, they also demonstrate how material units offer alternative formal, spatial, and organizational potentials—an aspect of his work that has clear echoes in contemporary practice.

With a gracious demeanor toward the interpretations cast onto his work by others, myself included, Lundy is steadfast about his process and to the medium in which he finds himself most comfortable: he is an expert draftsman. Lundy has spent a lifetime drawing; his early talents singled him out in many contexts, including the military, where they were put to productive ends. Conceiving of them less as a conduit for pictorial translation, for Lundy, drawings produce effects through the very imprint of their representational

Fig. 1 First Unitarian Church, Westport, Connecticut, skylight, 1961

grain: the granular markings of charcoal, the striated texture of a pencil's lineaments, or the light that emanates from color. Put together conceptually, these techniques produce extraordinary sketches, like the canonical one of the First Unitarian Church in Westport, where the conventional reliance on architectural specification seems pale in relation to the space, light, and figure that emerge as Lundy's charcoal markings erupt toward the sky; raw, gestural, and even imprecise, the sketch acquires a tectonic specificity as it records the striations of beams, planks, and the natural grain of the wood. In Lundy's work, the sketch takes on a constructive role, communicating things about fabrication that sometimes even a working drawing cannot achieve. This capability becomes even more important in projects like the Herron House, whose columns refuse organic resolution; the stacked wood grain of the laminated veneer lumber members is constructively composed to run parallel to the geometry of the roof vault in its center bay. However, since the house's side bays cantilever outwards as well, Lundy runs beams with conflicting grains that coalesce at the junction of the two vaults. This collision of grains is at the core of what his drawings for the project convey.

Between Lundy's deep disciplinary understanding of geometry, an intuition for structure, an interest in the technologies of production, and patient engagement with the craft of different trades, Lundy's career displays a virtuosity that is deeply architectural. He appealed to the technologies of his time, and yet his way of engaging them now seems almost anachronistic: he did with analog technologies what many could not do with today's sophisticated software.

Lundy's built work denies signature in the form of a singular voice; he lets the natural grain of raw matter, the texture of its aggregation, and the malleability of different materials help determine the aesthetic sensibility of his buildings. Consider the Unitarian Meeting House in Hartford, Connecticut, or the IBM Garden State Offices, in Cranford, New Jersey, and how Lundy negotiates history, identity, and building configuration through material organization. At the meeting house, while the structural frame of the building is composed of concrete fins and wood infill, both materials acquire an ancillary reading in relationship to the steel cables that are suspended as catenary rods overhead, giving

form to the space of worship. Playing with weight and lightness, Lundy undermines the traditional primacy of the structure by designing a tent-like awning, the levity of its radial organization offering a completely new reading for the church as rotunda. Lundy's plan reveals a deep underlying knowledge of history, but in guiding us through the material organization of the steel rods, with their delicate cadence, it forces us to recognize in the ghost of the building the transformation of the rotunda as building type.

So too, in the facade of the IBM project, we discover the power of the individual in the context of the collective. In this curious wall, Lundy adopts each brick as its own soldier with independent orders, and as each takes on its own position within the face of the building, we come to understand the power of the field condition as the basis for a compositional swarm. He blurs the relationship between the facade and the ground, allowing the brick to slip out from under the wall in increments, merging into the surface of the ground. From rustication at the wall's base to the lightening of orders at its top, Lundy constructs a dialogue with the classical facade and its tectonic hierarchies through a fluid geometry that dematerializes the very unit of brick in a gradient fashion. Lundy operates with great technical precision, but more importantly, through material mastery, he is also building a precise experience through the effects of the material behavior.

While architectural representation is dedicated to the illustration of possible realities, it is most commonly done as a pictorial act; contrary to this dictum, Lundy constructs his drawings as if building the representation on the page: line by line, and layer by layer. Lundy brings this metaphor for the precision entailed in the art of architecture to actuality, as he "builds" drawings on the one hand, and, on the other, allows his constructed buildings to gain perceptual resonance and ambiguity through light, weight, and tectonic play—the very qualities that might be easy for a drawing to suggest, but immensely difficult to fabricate. Somehow, Lundy masters both drawing and building, and these dual abilities make him less prone to easy characterization. In great part, this may be why Lundy did not achieve a wider audience during his career, but in hindsight he offers a paradigmatic position that is an outlier to common practices, something critical for historical reconsideration.

Fig. 2 IBM Garden State Office Building, Cranford, New Jersey, 1964

Preface

Donna Kacmar

Midcentury architect Victor Lundy designed civic buildings, churches, houses, and commercial buildings that show his awareness of materiality and structural form, and his ability to design with light and evoke the spirit of the time. He was educated in both the Beaux-Arts and Bauhaus schools of architecture, enabling him to combine his exceptional traditional drawing skills with modern space-making strategies. His schooling was interrupted by his service in World War II and a study tour of postwar Europe, after which he started his own firm in Sarasota, Florida. Later, he moved his practice to New York City, and then Texas, where he has lived ever since. During his career, Lundy designed buildings all over the world. While he spent many years working on larger buildings for the now-worldwide architecture firm HKS, this book concentrates on the smaller-scale projects Lundy executed independently while running his own practice.

An avid traveler and sketcher, Lundy documents the people and places he encounters as a way to understand the world and respond to it. His interest and abilities in drawing came early in childhood and were augmented with classes in painting and sculpture. As an adult, he often designed buildings during the day and painted at night. His son, Nicholas Lundy, writes of him:

My father is someone whose work, both in making architecture and art, is not only the dominant factor in his life, but also an extension of himself that can only be expressed through those mediums. My memories of my father when I was young always involve art making. He didn't have hobbies that didn't involve his art. When he wasn't at his office, he was sketching, making watercolors, painting, or sculpting. I think it is the way he truly expresses himself, and his work is perhaps an attempt to communicate something about himself that he's unable to in other ways. It has poured out of him for over seventy years undimmed in huge blasts of energy and resolve.[1]

I first met Lundy through friends and then slowly became more familiar with his life and work. A conference in Florida gave me the chance to visit his early projects in Sarasota, and the energy and enthusiasm embedded in them were clearly visible to me. The first time I saw *Victor Lundy: Sculptor of Space*, a 2014 documentary by the US General Services Administration (GSA) on his life and accomplishments, I was struck by the absence of any book about his work. I set about fixing that. My work began in earnest in the spring of 2016, when I accompanied Lundy to the Library of Congress in Washington, DC, to visit the archives

Fig. 1 Space Flowers, New York World's Fair, Flushing Meadows, New York, 1964

of his drawings, travel sketchbooks, and journals known as "brains books." I soon met many architects, historians, and scholars who have been equally intrigued by his work. This book is a collaborative effort between the many who want to share Lundy's work with others.

The foreword by Nader Tehrani, dean of the Cooper Union's Irwin S. Chanin School of Architecture and founding partner of the Boston firm NADAAA, makes the case for the relevancy of Lundy's work for contemporary architects.

An original essay, penned for this publication by Lundy, begins this book and is followed by my introduction.

C. Ford Peatross, the founding director of the Center for Architecture, Design, and Engineering (ADE) in the Prints and Photographs Division of the Library of Congress, acquired Lundy's archives for the Library of Congress in 2009. Peatross's essay describes Lundy's artistic talents from an early age, his Beaux-Arts and Bauhaus architectural training, and how his speed in graphic communication allowed him to test ideas and develop the design of buildings expediently.

Christopher S. Wilson, who teaches architecture and design history at Ringling College of Art and Design, narrates the time Lundy spent living and working in Sarasota, designing buildings known for their organic forms, swooping roofs, and playful masonry.

Christopher Domin, an architect and educator, is the coauthor (with Joseph King) of *Paul Rudolph: The Florida Houses* and lectures internationally on regional modernism and technological innovation. Domin writes about Lundy's influential churches, which are characterized by their expressive roofs and structure.

Joan M. Brierton and Sarah A. Garner, historic preservation specialists at GSA, worked on the production team for *Victor Lundy: Sculptor of Space*, the first comprehensive effort to document Lundy's life and legacy. Their essay examines the monumental US Tax Court Building in Washington, DC, which Lundy describes as the culminating work of his career.

The US Embassy in Colombo, Sri Lanka, was a true study in patience and determination. While he was awarded the initial design contract before the Tax Court project, the final design and working documents of the embassy weren't started until after the Tax Court Building was completed. Lundy jokes that he was able to "fast-track a 60,000 square foot office building in a mere twenty-three-year timeframe."[2] My essay on the embassy project describes how Lundy's seven trips to Colombo, numerous cuts to budget and scope, and multiple design iterations led to siting the building with full awareness of its connections to place and its importance to the people of Sri Lanka.

Stephen Fox, an architectural historian, a lecturer at the Rice School of Architecture and the Gerald D. Hines College of Architecture and Design at the University of Houston, and a fellow of the Anchorage Foundation of Texas, presents Lundy's more recent independent work, including houses and studios in Houston.

My concluding essay, "Sculpting Space," discusses how Lundy spent his career analyzing the basic elements of architecture—materials, structure, and light—to sculpt space. His work—while rooted in the time of its making—still resonates today and offers contemporary architects lessons on how to deeply investigate material choices, integrate structure with space, and bring light into spaces in order to elevate the experience of the inhabitants. It is my hope that this book, the first book focused solely on Lundy, will introduce his work to a new generation of architects and inspire future investigations into other aspects of his broad contributions to the art of architecture.

Fig. 2 Shade Structure at the Museum of History and Technology (now the National Museum of American History), Smithsonian, Washington, DC, 1965

On Design

Designing a building out of nothingness is akin to leading a great orchestra of disparate talent and virtuosity to the achievement of a monumental event in music. Or perhaps it is more like composing a piece of music out of crushing silence, hearing the components, fusing it all together.

In my work I've never gotten over the importance of "beginnings," ingrained in me in my early education in the Beaux-Arts system. The teachers would put you in little cubicles during the esquisse stages of a project. You were compelled to make a building "out of the blue" in a few hours, fix it conceptually in plan, section, and massing—and be linked inextricably to that concept for all the subsequent months of execution and development. There is an elemental power in spontaneity, in the first creative impressions and responses to an opportunity to build, to create, and to imagine something worthy out of the blank of a bare site.

The first thing I do is experience the site, feel it, become saturated in it, and absorb all the forces at work, energizing it, affecting it. Where is the sun in all of this? The rain, the clouds? How might the program context, the topography, the place's history, and unknown but anticipated events influence and affect the possibilities for the future of the site?

It is the sculptor in me that asks what I want the building form to be like: what is this emptiness asking for based on what tangible things I can see and know at the start? I begin a process of questioning right away, working from the outside in while engaging with what the building wants to be from the inside out.

Drawing is an integral part of how I work, and has been all my life. I draw better than I talk. When I "talk" my architecture or ideas, nothing happens. I am like an artisan—like a guy throwing clay pots. Things happen for me when I start drawing—when I start making lines and symbols. I do my architecture that way. I draw as I think, drawing on top of drawing. Drawing is a living experience, a participatory changing thing. A single stroke, a single mark, can change everything, like the spark of a thought.

I also make clay models at the start of each project, as an adjunct to visualizing a building in three dimensions. Working with Roma Plastilina in conjunction with my drawings lets me make changes and try out different concepts and forms. I love the smell and feel of Roma Plastilina and associate it with beginnings. I refine the irreducible image in clay.

Architecture is the largest art—it is sculpture in that the architect, in his or her final choices, determines the exterior image(s) from a distance, in silhouette. He or she decides how forms hit the ground—in masses, in wall forms, or raised on columns, or pins, facades intended or not, walls punctured by holes, masses, solids, and voids. The architect must resist making meaningless, mindless forms, fixing them and forcing plans unnaturally into preconceived shapes or envelopes. How is architecture perceived? It is never static like a photograph or a frozen architectural elevation. For a pedestrian in motion, volumes change, move, and hide other volumes; voids appear. Architecture is a changing, living experience.

As an architect, I have always been involved from the start in the systems that help give form and life to a complex project—the realm of structural engineering and the theory behind its design, the order of intelligent mechanical systems, and the intellectual discipline, all of which give sinews, muscle, and bone to form, and without which can lead to the proliferation of arbitrary decisions.

Because of the restraints of budget and time, most projects have to be accomplished through an honest process of communication and through choices based on creative, intelligent, inspired selection, a distillation that rises above passing fancy or freezing momentary inspiration. When works are truly fine, they have an inevitability about them, as if they weren't really "designed" at all but "happened" in some magic way.

I see architecture as the sublime art, and it is a sacred trust to be able to leave behind records of this highest order of creativity. As it says on the frieze of the American Academy of Arts and Letters, "All Passes Art Alone Untiring Stays to Us."

At a period in American history beset with cynicism, open scrutiny, and examination of the basic structure of American systems, design offers an opportunity for reaffirmation, a chance to create true American symbols. It seems a wonderful time to make building statements of true worth, whose values reassure and reach far beyond the current scene.

Victor Lundy, FAIA
Bellaire, Texas
October 11, 2017

The Life and Work of Victor Lundy

Donna Kacmar

Victor Lundy is one of a small generation of American architects trained first in the Beaux-Arts tradition at New York University and later introduced to the Bauhaus principles at Harvard. Lundy began his career amid the spirit of optimism that permeated the United States after World War II. The subsequent burst of construction activity and growth in the suburbs led to a wide acceptance of modernism in the communities in which he worked. His practice, based first in Sarasota, Florida, and later in New York City and Houston, ranged from small-scale residential and commercial buildings to expressive religious structures, and included his two preeminent institutional works: the US Tax Court Building in Washington, DC, and the US Embassy in Sri Lanka.

Lundy was born to Russian immigrants in a New York City brownstone on February 1, 1923. His father was a gifted musician who had won an important piano competition in Russia before Victor was born. His mother, Rachel, was highly intelligent and striking (figs. 2–3). She was a perceptive woman and a dedicated mentor to her son. He confirms, "I owe whatever I am to her."[1]

Times were hard in New York during the Great Depression, and Lundy's father, Alfred, shoveled snow in Central Park to help support the family. Given these difficult circumstances, Lundy's father could not resist an enticing Russian program to induce talented émigrés back to their home country. The family moved to Russia when Victor was a young boy. That turned out to be a short-lived stay—after just one year in what is now Saint Petersburg, the Lundys rushed back to the United States, with a brief stop to visit family in Belgium in 1934, before their visas expired. This ended his father's music career, and the family became "Americans forever"[2] (fig. 4).

Lundy's fascination and ability with drawing became evident quite early, when an elementary school art teacher asked each student to color a circle as evenly as possible. Lundy remembers:

> I've always known the importance of striving to make a perfect thing. I still remember my first such sense of accomplishment—was I five, or six?—and the first-grade exercise of coloring a circle to make a perfect orange. I was driven to stay flawlessly within the line, to make the orange color spectacularly uniform with my crayon. I expected praise and it came.[3]

When his teacher saw the beautifully rendered circle, she told Lundy's parents, "This kid is something."[4] That incident

Fig. 1 Lundy House and Studio, Aspen, Colorado

Fig. 2 Victor Lundy's mother, Rachel (Yulia), 1920
Fig. 3 Victor with Rachel, 1923

was the first indication of his future talents. His mother continued to support and encourage his artistic skills, and drawing and painting eventually became integral to his architectural work.

At his six-thousand-student, all-boy public high school in New York City, Lundy was known as the "school's artist."[5] His English teacher predicted that young Lundy would become either an artist or an actor. He went to New York University on a full scholarship and began to take classes in the College of Arts and Science. He later transferred to the NYU School of Architecture and Applied Arts within the College of Fine Arts to study architecture. The school was known for its sophisticated Beaux-Arts program, headed by the well-known professor Georges Gromort (1870–1961), who had taught at the École des Beaux-Arts in Paris before joining NYU in 1928. Lundy was smitten by this introduction to architecture. His coursework included watercolor, pencil drawing, charcoal drawing, and perspective, as well as differential and integral calculus, advanced French, and real estate. He had received over two years of architectural training by the time Pearl Harbor was attacked on December 7, 1941.

Lundy volunteered, first in the air force, and then earned advanced acceptance in the new Army Specialized Training Program (ASTP), established to produce officers to lead the reconstruction of Europe after the war. He was sent to the University of Maine and was pleased to take courses in structural and mechanical engineering. After eight months there, the ASTP was abandoned, and all soldiers in the program were immediately transferred to infantry replacement divisions and sent off to Europe. Lundy readily admits that the ASTP was a group of "pretty smart guys" who were thrust into a world of combat without enough proper training as frontline infantrymen[6] (fig. 5).

Lundy became a Browning automatic rifleman in the army, joining Company K of the 104th Infantry Regiment, 26th Yankee Division, on maneuvers in Tennessee. On August 27, 1944, after completing basic training, he was shipped overseas for combat in France.

Lundy served as a frontline combat infantry sergeant in General George Patton's Third Army, participating in campaigns in northern France and the Rhineland. Lundy continued to draw throughout the war, sometimes even drawing while walking with a pack on his back. He carried three-by-five-inch spiral-bound sketchbooks with him to document villages, buildings, fellow soldiers, and whatever else caught his eye. Everyone knew Lundy had studied architecture before the war, and one day, a fellow soldier told him, "You might be interested in this German soldier we captured."[7] Lundy became friendly with the captured officer, an architect, who updated him on the latest architectural news, including that Gropius was now chairman of the Department of Architecture at Harvard and that the modernist German architect Ludwig Mies van der Rohe (1886–1969), who had been a director at the Bauhaus, was now at the Illinois Institute of Technology in Chicago. These conversations reignited Lundy's interest in completing his architectural education and his subsequent interest in attending Harvard to learn from the modernist architects once the conflict was over.

Before his architectural education could continue, Lundy experienced firsthand the violence of war. He was wounded in action and later awarded the Purple Heart, Combat Infantryman Badge First Award, Bronze Star Medal, Good Conduct Medal, European-African-Middle Eastern Campaign Medal with two bronze service stars, and World War II Victory Medal.

In November 1944 he was hit by heavy German artillery that opened on American positions in Rodalbe in Alsace-Lorraine. The Americans, after already taking control of two nearby towns, heard German infantry and tanks coming their way. Sergeant Lundy ordered the soldiers "into the cellar!"[8] of the nearest stone house. He was the last one down the stairs. As he looked back, he saw a German Tiger tank and soldiers crashing in between two houses just twenty feet away, their 88-millimeter artillery gun lowering to aim in his direction. As he slammed the cast-iron door closed, his right side was protected but his left side was exposed. The force of the shell burst through the door, hitting Lundy. His left arm flew up in the air, and, thinking he had lost it, he grabbed at it with his right arm, happy to find it still there. But he had been hit and fell to the ground twitching, seriously wounded in his left hand, elbow, and side. A fellow soldier yelled, "Vic, get up! Get up! Follow me," probably saving his life. German soldiers were just outside and approaching rapidly. He stumbled away from town in the snow, in the direction of the tank support camp. Hearing the voices of soldiers, he was relieved to find that they were Americans. He followed them, with no one helping him. When he came across barbed wire fences, he had to throw his whole body over to get through, cutting his skin. The soldiers finally reached tank support, and Lundy later

Fig. 4 Victor, with his sister Nora (left) and cousin (right), Antwerp, Belgium, ca. 1934
Fig. 5 Victor with his parents, Atlantic City, New Jersey, 1943

Fig. 6 Watercolor from Lundy's travels on the Rotch Travelling Scholarship, Saltsjöbaden, Sweden, 1948

learned that he was one of only 16 in his battalion of 350 who were neither captured nor killed.[9]

After a brief stay in a Parisian hospital, Lundy was sent to the American hospital in Stourport-on-Severn, north of Birmingham, England. His new doctor was a major who always had cookies in his pocket, wore his hat backward, and called Lundy "sonny boy." He noticed Lundy's sketchbooks and said, "I have been waiting for someone like you to draw surgeries."[10] That doctor, Hampar Kelikian (1899–1983), a well-known orthopedic surgeon from Chicago, had perfected an operation for soldiers who had lost their thumbs. He first repaired the wound by cutting a U-shaped piece from the soldier's chest and attaching the flap to the hand. Shifting the position of the index finger and connecting it to healthy ligaments allowed the hand to grip and hold using the "new thumb" formed from the index finger. Lundy attended all surgeries and did drawings in situ of this new procedure. Kelikian also operated on Lundy's hand and elbow. The doctor kept Lundy there for several months doing drawings and made sure that he was sent to Walter Reed Army Medical Center in Washington, DC, for a full recovery.

Lundy had multiple surgeries during the eight months he spent at Walter Reed. After he recovered from a bone graft surgery that took a sliver of bone from his right shin to replace the missing one inch of bone in his left hand, Lundy felt certain that he would soon be discharged. During his convalescence period he retrieved his architecture books from his mother and went, in his army uniform, to Harvard to meet with Gropius. Lundy applied to Harvard and even rented a room at Mount Auburn Place in Cambridge.

Back at Walter Reed, he went to his final interview and examination. His doctor, Nicholas Capos, had recently been transferred, so Lundy met with a new doctor, who regarded Lundy coldly through his rimless eyeglasses. Their dislike was mutual and immediate. When asked how he felt, Lundy responded, "Great," as in "great and ready for civilian life." But Lundy was sent back to active duty at Camp Upton, the very same camp to which he had been assigned when he first enlisted. He needed eighty-five points for his Advanced Service Rating Score to be eligible for discharge, and Lundy only had seventy-eight. The army had a serious shortage of manpower for the planned invasion of Japan, and he now was an experienced replacement frontline infantry sergeant, about to be shipped to the Pacific theater.

When Lundy called his mother to let her know he was being sent to the Pacific, she burst into tears and asked if he could get a "vacation."[11] He finagled a one-week furlough and returned to New York City, where he stayed out late every night going to dance halls and drinking. Each morning his mother asked if he had had a good time, and each night she sent him back out to have fun and do all his living before he went back to the war.

During that furlough week in August 1945, the United States dropped atomic bombs on Hiroshima and Nagasaki. Through this act, President Harry Truman saved an enormous number of American lives, and he remains a hero to Lundy to this day. On V-J Day, Lundy's mother raised a window of the apartment and tore up the phone book, tossing the pages into the wind. Lundy went to Times Square and kissed "anything that moved."[12] He was released from active duty on October 11, 1945.

He had already been admitted to Harvard and arrived two months into the semester. He remembers walking into Robinson Hall as an infantry veteran, wearing his uniform, to find his fellow students standing on the drafting tables, having a clay fight. He was now about to learn from Bauhaus masters and was placed in the advanced design class with the Hungarian-born Breuer, who had studied and taught at the Bauhaus with Gropius. Lundy showed Breuer, an architect, his wartime sketchbooks and an oil painting. Breuer said, "If you get to doing architecture at the level you can draw…we will see what you can do."[13]

Lundy's earlier Beaux-Arts training influenced how he worked. He rendered his first project at Harvard in the same style as the last project at New York University, working secretively in his dormitory room at Dunster House. For his final submission, he covered four entire walls with giant color paintings on casein paper. The other students produced black-and-white ink drawings. He was lucky to pass the assignment, and immediately bought German pens and began to draw in the Bauhaus style, making black-and-white ink drawings for his subsequent projects.

Harvard boasted many future architectural icons among its students, including the Austrian-born Australian architect Harry Seidler (1923–2006) and the American Paul Rudolph (1918–1997). Rudolph, who later became the chair of the Department of Architecture at Yale University, was considered the "hot shot," but Lundy felt that he made Rudolph nervous. Lundy recalls inviting Rudolph to his atelier and thinking to himself, "I will show him something better than anything he has ever done."[14]

During the war, Lundy had not thought much about women, being preoccupied with survival. When he returned to the United States, his sister began introducing him to available women. While an undergraduate student, he met Shirley Corwin (1925–2012), who was then a French translator at the United Nations, and they married in 1947 and moved to a Beacon Hill basement apartment. Lundy received his bachelor of architecture degree in 1947 and was accepted by Gropius for one more year of study. In 1948 Lundy received his master of architecture degree.

At Harvard, Lundy was known for his presentations and renderings. His skills were showcased when he applied for and was awarded the Rotch Travelling Scholarship by the Boston Society of Architects.[15] The scholarship, the oldest of its kind in the country, was founded in 1883, and allows young American architects to travel to study art and architecture. Lundy also received the Edward Kendall Scholarship from Harvard, and the combined scholarships allowed him and Shirley to spend eighteen months traveling through postwar Europe and elsewhere overseas. He honors Shirley for her adept management of their limited funds, which supported their extended travel.

From July 1948 until January 1950, the couple toured England, Germany, Sweden, Denmark, Finland, the Netherlands, Belgium, France, Liechtenstein, Austria, Switzerland, Monaco, Italy, Greece, Turkey, Syria, Lebanon, Egypt, Spain, Morocco, Algeria, and Tunisia. Lundy carried a small watercolor pad to capture street scenes and buildings during short stops on the train or bus (fig. 6). He also completed more finished paintings on an eighteen-by-twenty-four-inch Arches Cold Press Watercolor Pad.

Before his travels, Gropius and others provided Lundy with sealed letters of introduction to European architects who might assist him in his travels. Despite Gropius's praise of his sketches, Lundy neglected to bring his sketchbooks to his appointment with Le Corbusier (1887–1965) at 35 rue de Sèvres in Paris, where he arrived to find the older architect in an unfriendly mood. "It was a big deal and sort of intimidating," Lundy says. "I thought 'oh, come now, that is showing too much ego, to bring your sketchbooks.' It was a big mistake…"[16] Though their meeting was inauspicious, it was Lundy's subsequent visit to the Salvation Army building that had a greater impact: the project made such a negative impression on Lundy that it dissuaded him from visiting other modern buildings. Instead, he sought out traditional architecture in the more than three hundred cities he visited

as a Rotch scholar. Years later Lundy recalls, "I remember how my eighteen months abroad on the Rotch changed my life, and I envy now the time I had then. It sustained me for ten years."[17]

Lundy had gained some experience working in architectural firms during the summers of 1941 and 1942, on breaks between his studies at NYU. After receiving his bachelor's degree from Harvard, he worked at Kaufmann, Lippincott, and Eggers in Los Angeles, where his parents had moved from New York City. While completing his graduate work, he worked for one of his Harvard professors, Walter Bogner (1899–1993). Upon returning to the United States, Lundy was not sure where he wanted to settle. He decided to go back to New York City, where he took (and passed) the architectural licensing exam on November 5, 1950. A project soon took him to Sarasota, Florida, prompting him to move south for the ample opportunities it presented for young architects.

Lundy's first building design in the Sarasota area was a small project in Venice, a few miles south of Sarasota. He had read in the *Sarasota Herald Tribune* about a "drive-in" outdoor church. The congregation had a wonderful site but no building, so services were held for parishioners as they sat in their cars. Lundy introduced himself to the Reverend Robert White and offered to design an inexpensive structure that would lift him up in the air so he could be seen. In addition to Lundy's talents, this pro bono project benefited from a wonderful builder who was frugal with the congregation's limited construction budget of $3,000. When *Life* magazine featured a story on the project, the spread included a picture of a young couple in a convertible: Lundy's family.[18]

Soon after his arrival in Sarasota, Lundy entered and won a watercolor competition, and those watercolor skills led directly to his first paid architectural commission. Karl Bickel (1882–1972), who had recently retired from his role as president of the United Press International, was one of the jurors of that competition, and when he discovered that Lundy was also an architect, Bickel asked him to do a few sketches for a new Chamber of Commerce building. Lundy went to the site with a giant easel and produced four large paintings that won him the commission. The building exists today and has been nicknamed "The Blue Pagoda" for the color of the roof tiles, imported from Seoul, South Korea.

Lundy's former classmate Rudolph was already well established in Sarasota when Lundy arrived, which made it harder for the latter to get a foothold there. Lundy focused

Fig. 7 Victor Lundy, Sarasota, Florida, 1960

on his work to alleviate feelings of vulnerability. While there was no "Sarasota School" per se, there was, at that time, a group of energetic young architects who were able to develop their practices with an enlightened and rather fearless clientele.

In Sarasota, as Lundy's commissions grew, his work began to earn publication and recognition. Lundy was the youngest "creative" to be invited by Don MacKinnon, director of the Institute of Personality Assessment and Research at the University of California, Berkeley, to participate in a creativity study in 1959. The three-day-long assessments of Louis Kahn, Philip Johnson, I. M. Pei, Eero Saarinen, and others were intended to find the relationship between personality, environment, and creativity.[19] But even as he was becoming well known, he was passed over, as a "local" architect, for consideration to design the Hamilton Center at New College of Florida. Lundy realized that he needed to leave Sarasota to earn larger commissions. After practicing in Florida for eight years, he moved his office back

to New York City, but continued doing work in Sarasota (fig. 7). He and his employees often shuttled between the two offices. Boyd Blackner, a former employee, shares his insight on the office:

> Lundy worked in prodigious bursts—all night, weekends, in hotel rooms, and on planes. He produced superb, huge drawings, dripping with ink, watercolor, oils, charcoal, crayon, and pastels. Clay models that weighed fifty pounds would emerge from his office on the other side of the hall. All of these were true works of art that combined schematics, preliminaries and design development into one Plastiline phase. Also, there were sketch books filled with quotes from the client, impressions of the site, poetic searches for the essence of the project, design sketches, details, program areas and relationships, budgets, schedules, calculations, specification items and instructions. He would even come in and letter finish schedules and title blocks late into the night if deadlines were really desperate.[20]

Not only was Lundy energetic in his practice, but he thoroughly examined each project program and site. He worked to understand the needs of all the building users, often interviewing multiple people, even for building types with which he had previous experience. He was always searching for new ways to understand a problem and spent time documenting a site's landscape, trees, and other contextual influences. For instance, at the US Embassy in Sri Lanka, Lundy wrote about the site's political importance and its physical features in a report to the State Department.[21] Synthesizing this information, he intuitively developed creative solutions while using the architect's tools—material, structure, and light—in a sophisticated way. In a talk he gave at Ball State University, Lundy remarked, "Architecture is not for amateurs."[22]

In 1960, amid significant changes in his personal life—he and Shirley divorced and he married his second wife, Anstis Burwell (1924–2009)—Lundy's office was particularly busy (figs. 8–9). He was working on two residences in Sarasota, as well as a church, an office building, the Frontenac Hotel in Florida, the Hillspoint School in Westport, Connecticut, and the design of the South American traveling exhibit for the US Atomic Energy Commission. Over the next ten years, Lundy designed projects as diverse as the I. Miller Showroom on Fifth Avenue in Manhattan; the Sierra Blanca Ski Resort near Ruidoso, New Mexico; pavilions for the World's

Fig. 8 Victor Lundy on a train to Venice, Italy, August 1964

Fig. 9 Anstis Burwell Lundy on a train to Venice, Italy, August 1964

Fair; the IBM Garden State Office Building; and the Intermediate School 53 in Far Rockaway, Queens, New York.

The pace and size of the commissions continued to increase until his two major projects at the time, the US Tax Court Building and the US Embassy in Ceylon (now Sri Lanka), were put on hold during the Vietnam War. The contract for these two large and high-profile public projects changed the general nature of the work in his office at the time. I can only speculate that, had his work continued with church and small-scale private commercial projects, the impact of the war on his office might have been reduced.

This downturn of his office workload gave Lundy time to design and build a house in Aspen for himself and Anstis, a talented watercolor artist. The Lundy House and Studio in Aspen, a compact volume set in a natural landscape, has full-height glass with ample space for painting easels. The double-height living room space is capped with a faceted-wood ceiling and focuses on a large brick fireplace with a raised hearth. The sophisticated roof structural system is balanced by the simplicity of the solid, double-Wythe brick enclosing walls to create a light-filled, serene space (fig. 1, page 16, and figs. 10–11). Later, after they moved to Houston, Anstis spent summers at the house she loved, painting and escaping the summer heat, while Lundy worked incessantly back in Texas.

Lundy began to teach in order to survive the economic ebbs and flows affecting his small architectural practice, and, in 1975, he headed to California Polytechnic State University in San Luis Obispo. Lundy started teaching at the University of Houston in 1976 after an auspicious social meeting with University of Houston president Barry Munitz in Aspen. A former student recalls Lundy telling his students, "For God's sake people, design something worth building!"[23] While Lundy was teaching, the US Embassy project was rekindled in 1976, and he soon opened his Houston office. Victor A. Lundy & Associates, Inc. was incorporated in 1979 and Lundy stopped teaching in 1984.

After completing the working drawings for the embassy, Lundy entered into a partnership in Houston with Harwood Taylor. The small firm worked with HKS, a large Dallas firm, to help with construction administration of projects. This led indirectly to Lundy being hired, after his partnership with Taylor ended, by Ron Brame, president of HKS, to serve as design principal (fig. 12). Lundy flew to Dallas every Monday and back home to Houston on Friday. Bryan Trubey, then a thirty-year-old architect and now a principal at HKS, worked one desk away from Lundy and recalls, "I saw him doing breathtaking work."[24] James Atkins, former CEO of HKS, describes Lundy as a "true artist" and recalls how Lundy was humble and fun yet "serious as hell when it comes to

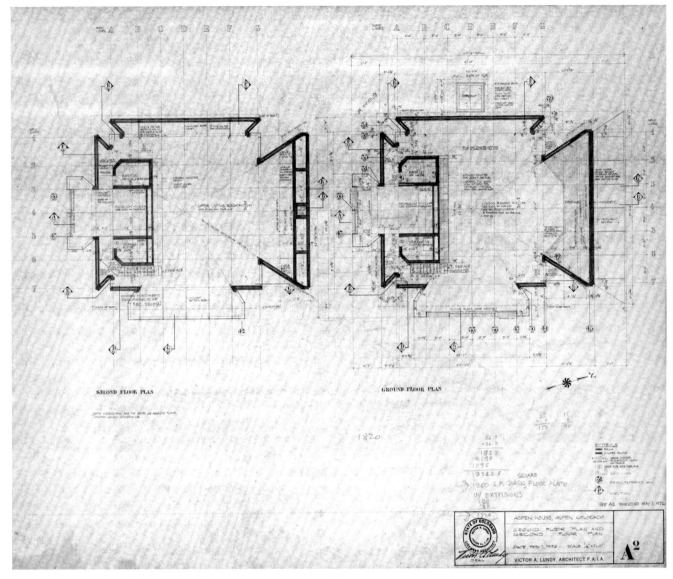

Fig. 10 Lundy House and Studio, Aspen, Colorado, ground and second floor plans, February 1, 1972

design."[25] Atkins remembers that once, when intensely focused on a project, Lundy taped paper to the glass walls of his office so no one would see his designs and announced, "I'm keeping the doors locked, just throw me meat."[26]

At HKS Lundy worked on large office complexes such as the Austin Centre and One Congress Plaza in Austin and the Walnut Glen Tower and GTE Telephone Operations World Headquarters in Dallas. The nine-story Austin Centre includes an office tower, hotel, and condominiums organized around a central enclosed atrium. The structure is clearly expressed, with the exterior wall pulled back away from the columns at an angle to reveal the building systems, as well

as provide additional corner windows. The former GTE building (now Verizon) in Las Colinas, just north of Dallas, began as an invited competition between HKS, Pei Cobb Freed, KPF, and DSA. Early sketches by Lundy show the incorporation of outdoor spaces with the building masses on the 2.4-million-square-foot campus. Lundy also worked on many competitions and other large projects that were not built, including a very progressive eighty-story speculative office tower for Houston. The last built work he designed with HKS was the Jon L. Hagler Center for the Texas A&M University Foundation in College Station, Texas, completed in 1999.

Fig. 11 Lundy House and Studio, Aspen, Colorado, facing east from living area

While working with others on much larger buildings, Lundy also continued designing smaller projects including a studio in Bellaire (a municipality within the Houston metropolitan area) for Anstis, and later, an addition to her studio that became the couple's home, where Lundy continues to live. Other works he designed in Houston included his own studio (1998) and the Joan Miller House (2003). In 2004 he also renovated a stone cottage in Marfa, Texas, for him and Anstis, giving it several signature Lundy details such as cantilevered glass shelves set in the stone walls and a faceted plywood ceiling reminiscent of the Aspen house ceiling. These smaller Texas projects connect more directly in scale to his work designed from his earlier offices in Sarasota and New York.

Although Lundy no longer practices architecture, his work continues to be appreciated. In 2006 Ballroom Marfa staged a joint exhibition titled *The Art and Architecture of Anstis and Victor Lundy* in Marfa, Texas. That same year, the *Beyond the Harvard Box* exhibition focused on the early built work of Harvard students, including Lundy, and was paired with a symposium in Cambridge. In 2014 the GSA produced the documentary *Victor Lundy: Sculptor of Space*. In 2014 both his Tax Court Building and his US Embassy in Sri Lanka were selected for inclusion in the US Pavilion at the Venice Biennale. And in November 2016 he was presented with the inaugural Sarasota Architecture Foundation Lifetime Achievement Award. Lundy currently lives in Bellaire, where he continues to draw and paint the world around him, extending the artistic skills that have sustained his work and life (fig. 13).

Fig. 12 (top) Victor Lundy at HKS, Dallas, Texas, with wood study model of One Congress, 1983

Fig. 13 (bottom) Victor Lundy, Bellaire, Texas, 2008

Artist Architect

C. Ford Peatross

The line between artist and architect is uniquely and often exquisitely blurred in Victor Lundy's work. This chapter explores a portion of his rich and extensive archive held in the Victor A. Lundy Archive at the Library of Congress. The archive includes a small group of examples of his formative work as a student; tens of thousands of his preliminary, working, and presentation drawings as a professional architect; over two hundred of his uniquely informative and richly illustrated "brains books"; and hundreds of his often-ravishing travel drawings. The archive is supplemented further by thousands of Lundy's own photographs of his works and travels and professional photographs of his work.[1]

Drawing played very different roles for Lundy and his contemporaries. For Paul Rudolph, drawing was an all-consuming activity he engaged in so intensely that his favored white shirts and pants often were smeared with graphite and colored pencil. However innovative, imaginative, and even passionate, his drawings were almost exclusively an expression of his architectural designs. For I. M. Pei (1917–), drawing was a necessary tool for which he appears to have had no great fondness. Although intellectually and creatively distinguished, his drawings evidence little joy in their making. For Lundy, though, drawing was entirely another

matter. Starting in his youth, drawing and painting have been for him as necessary and natural as breathing, and have served as the primary expression not only of his architectural designs and interests but also of his world and his soul. He is a joyful and passionate worker, a traveler, and an observer and recorder of the world. Although the built environment is present in almost every aspect of his work, his acute skills of representation and observation are devoted to many subjects: nature, landscape, people, art, music, theories, ideas, opinions, and everyday experiences. His drawings and paintings reveal to us the inspirations, sources, processes, and quotidian practices and beliefs of an accomplished architect and an artist.

Lundy was an artist before he ever considered being an architect. His talents were evident at an early age, and at seventeen he produced an exactly realistic drawing of the head of a bull for an art class at DeWitt Clinton High School, precociously cropping his image in a highly original and unconventional manner[2] (fig. 2). During his two years of architecture study at New York University before World War II, Lundy was one of almost five hundred students in a program with a faculty of almost fifty architects, engineers, and other professionals. The curriculum was based partly on

Fig. 1 Sanctuary, St. Paul's Lutheran Church, Sarasota, Florida, 2006. Perspective rendering of the nave, carbon pencils and charcoal on paper, 48 x 96 inches

the practices of the French École des Beaux-Arts and was first organized in 1926 in collaboration with the Beaux-Arts Institute of Design in New York.[3] This was supplemented by courses in art and industrial design taught by prominent New York–based artists and designers such as Winold Reiss (1886–1953).[4] All of this provided Lundy with skills in design, drawing, composition, materials, and structure that proved useful throughout his career. In the words of the school's dean, E. Raymond Bossange, the students enjoyed "the additional advantage of studying in the most interesting city architecturally in the world today."[5]

The school's emphasis on both drawing and the history of architecture is evident in one of Lundy's student-exam drawings from a course in architectural history, a partially cutaway perspective sketch in which the general massing, rhythms, orders, and details of the Roman Coliseum are all recorded with graphic economy (fig. 3). The same Beaux-Arts drawing skills and interest in historical architecture are evident in one of the sketches from Lundy's World War II sketchbooks.[6] Done quickly, it nevertheless captures both the charm and the details of a vernacular Norman stone farmhouse near Crasville, France, that Lundy found exceptional (fig. 4).

As an architectural student at Harvard from 1945 to 1947, Lundy submitted presentation drawings for review by faculty members, including Walter Gropius, Hugh Stubbins, Marcel Breuer, and Walter Bogner. Lundy's archive includes photographic reproductions of two of these drawings, done for classes with Breuer, that demonstrate that proficiency. The first depicts an ambitious scheme for an automobile station and service center for the Gulf Oil company (fig. 5). The attenuated and sweeping perspective elevation substantially predates Ed Ruscha's famous *Standard Station* paintings and prints of the 1960s, but shares much of their drama and energy, with a tightly composed Breueresque main building featuring horizontal ribbons of windows and vertical cladding culminating with a streamlined automobile under a wafer-thin modernist canopy punctuated by V-shaped supports. An interior perspective depicts a luxurious, lofty, and spacious muraled interior sparsely populated with elegant furnishings and a curvaceous counter and display cabinets.

The second drawing, for a 1946 Harvard student competition for an "Expansible House," was done without the ink and watercolor washes of the Beaux-Arts style, a new

method of drawing for Lundy, both thoroughly modernist and also Breueresque in its design vocabulary (fig. 6). The drawing is, however, also very Beaux-Arts in the highly skilled composition of its varied elements: plans, elevations, details, and both an interior perspective and a bird's-eye exterior perspective view, including a landscaped site. Its organization recalls nothing so much as the popular "small house" competition drawings expertly composed by many Beaux-Arts trained architects prior to World War II. Breuer was impressed enough with Lundy's talents that he hired him the same year to work in his office and to produce a drawing for one of Breuer's own design commissions, contemporary with the master's own similar and widely published residence in New Canaan, Connecticut, of 1946–48.[7]

During Lundy's travels for the distinguished Rotch Travelling Scholarship between June 1948 and January 1950, he and his wife visited over twenty countries. During this time he was required to produce drawings of distinguished architectural sites and monuments, both historical and modern.[8] Primarily ink and watercolor drawings on paper, they are quite varied in their methods of representation and points of view. At the Luxor Temple in Egypt he placed the dark and almost abstractly rendered statue of a seated figure in the foreground with the glowing ruins of the temple in the distance (fig. 7). On the Athenian Acropolis he was "totally overwhelmed" by the noble sight of the Parthenon's peripteral colonnade of Pentelic marble, shimmering in the August heat and almost dissolving in his watery rendering[9] (fig. 8). He remembers of his sketch of Mont Saint-Michel in France that he "was quite taken with this long distance image and made this quick watercolor to capture the approach" (fig. 9).

As he began his professional practice in Florida in the 1950s, Lundy used his drawing skills to considerable advantage.[10] An exhibition in Sarasota that included one of his watercolors of Notre Dame Cathedral in Paris led to an offer to design the new building for the Sarasota Chamber of Commerce, featuring a large spreading roof clad in gleaming turquoise Asian tiles. For that commission, he produced a series of large-scale paintings showing the building completely at home in the semitropical setting provided by the adjacent botanical garden[11] (see page 56, fig. 4). Even when Lundy produced more traditional presentation drawings for a project, his graphic skills, imagination, and eagerness to

(continued on page 49)

Fig. 2 Drawing of a head of a bull, ca. 1939. Graphite on illustration board, 16 x 23 inches.

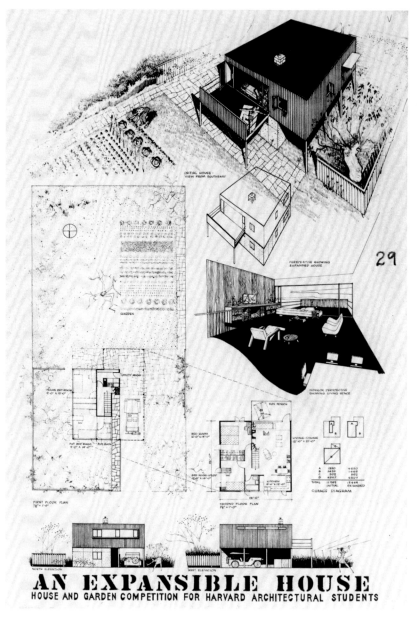

Fig. 3 (top left) "Hist. of Arch. Lecture #13, Sketch #2. Colosseum, Exterior," 1940–1941. Perspective sketch, ebony pencil on paper, 9 x 6 inches

Fig. 4 (middle left) "A house near Crasville, Normandy, France," page from Lundy's World War II sketchbook, 1944. Ebony pencil on paper, 5 x 3 inches

Fig. 5 (bottom left) Gulf automobile station and service center, Harvard student drawing, 1946. Original, ink on board, 36 x 24 inches. Negative photostatic copy, ca. 1946, 13.63 x 18.63 inches

Fig. 6 (right) "An Expansible House, House and Garden Competition for Harvard Architectural Students," 1946. Original, ink on board, 36 x 24 inches. Positive photostatic copy, 18.63 x 13.63 inches, ca. 1946

Fig. 7 (opposite) Statue and temple at Luxor, Egypt, from Lundy's travels on the Rotch Travelling Scholarship, September 1949. Watercolor and graphite on paper, 24 x 18 inches

Fig. 8 Parthenon, Greece, from Lundy's travels on the Rotch Travelling Scholarship, August 1949.
Watercolor and graphite, 18 x 24 inches

Fig. 9 Mont-Saint-Michel, Normandy, France, from Lundy's travels on the Rotch Travelling Scholarship, March 1949. Watercolor and graphite, 18 x 24 inches

Fig. 10 (above) St. Andrews Presbyterian Church, Dunedin, Florida, 1960. Presentation rendering, graphite, watercolor, and colored and metallic pencil on brown paper, 30 x 22 inches

PARKING STRUCTURE FOR THE STATE
STATE UNIVERSITY CONSTRUCTION

Fig. 11 Parking Structure for the State University of New York at Cortland State University, February 25, 1969.
Perspective rendering, A12, carbon pencils and charcoal on drafting film, 69 x 36 inches

VERSITY OF NEW YORK AT CORTLAND
D   VICTOR A. LUNDY, ARCHITECT FAIA, NEW YORK

NORTHWEST ELEVATION

SCALE: 1/8"=1'-0"
FEBRUARY 25, 1969

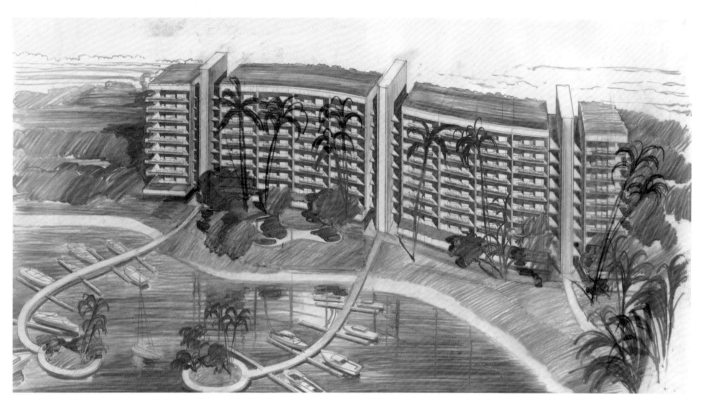

Fig. 12 (opposite, top) "Lucaya," Bradenton, Florida, for O. F. Smith Enterprises, Inc., 1973. Aerial perspective rendering, carbon pencils and charcoal on drafting film, 36 x 60 inches

Fig. 13 (opposite, bottom) Shade structures, Smithsonian Institution, Museum of History and Technology (now the National Museum of American History), Washington, DC, 1970. Perspective rendering, carbon pencils and charcoal on Mylar drafting film, 62 x 36 inches

Fig. 14 Hagler Foundation, College Station, Texas, 1997. Perspective rendering, watercolor and graphite, print from 4 x 5–inch color transparency

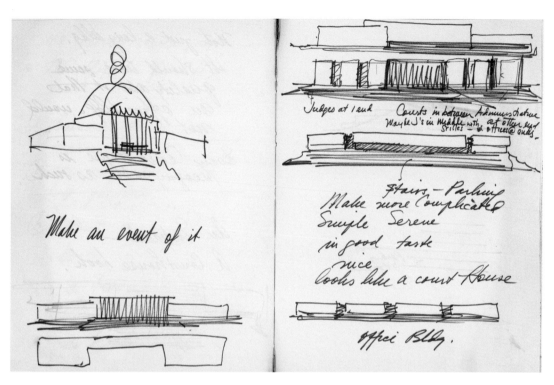

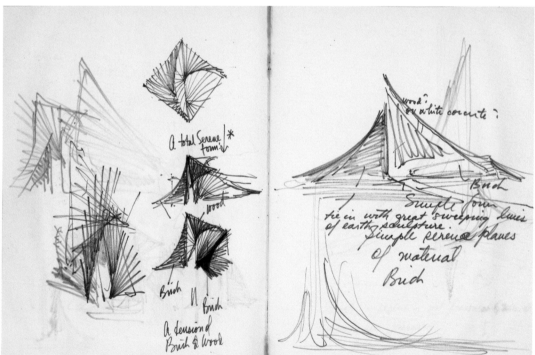

Fig. 15 (top) Concept sketches and comments concerning the US Tax Court building in Washington, DC, page from Lundy's brains books, 1965

Fig. 16 (bottom) Sketches and notes in response to lecture on "Structural Innovations in Masonry," page from Lundy's brains books, 1965

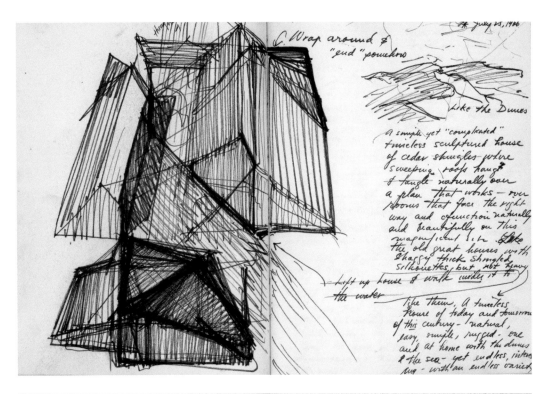

Fig. 17 (top) Concept and site sketches and notes, Ben Heller Residence, East Hampton, Long Island, New York, page from Lundy's brains books, July 25, 1966

Fig. 18 (bottom) Site sketch, Ben Heller Residence project, East Hampton, Long Island, New York, page from Lundy's brains books, July 25, 1966

Fig. 19 Courtyard, Prague Castle, framed by Jože Plečnik's Bull Staircase, from Lundy's travel sketchbook, ca. 1975. Craypas and color markers on Bristol paper, 18 x 48 inches

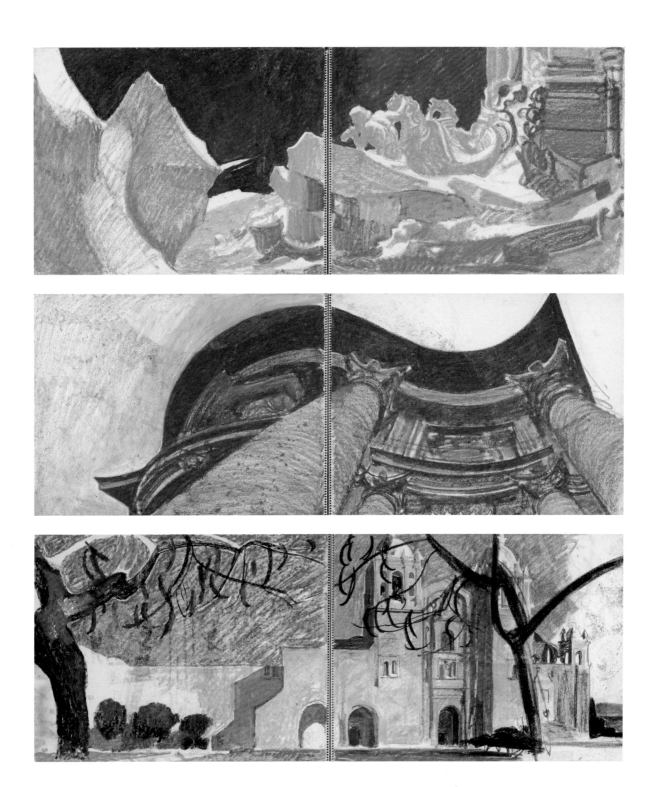

Fig. 20 (top) Trevi Fountain, Rome, from Lundy's travel sketchbook, ca. 1975. Craypas on Bristol paper, 18 x 48 inches

Fig. 21 (middle) Francesco Borromini's San Carlo alle Quattro Fontane, Rome, entrance detail from Lundy's travel sketchbook, ca. 1975. Craypas on Bristol paper, 18 x 48 inches

Fig. 22 (bottom) Church and former monastery of Santo Domingo de Guzmán, Oaxaca, Mexico, from Lundy's travel sketchbook, between 1974 and 2000 (exact date unknown). Craypas on paper, 18 x 48 inches

Fig. 23 (opposite) Entrance facade of a church near Nochistlán, Mexico, from Lundy's travel sketchbook, ca. 1975. Craypas on paper, 28 x 17 inches

make his ideas more accessible to his clients often led him to, as they say, "mix things up."

In 1960, to represent the swooping and audacious stone, wooden, and glazed forms of his unprecedented design for St. Andrews Presbyterian Church in Dunedin, Florida, his presentation drawings employed watercolor and multicolored and metallic pencils for the stained glass windows (fig. 10). They were drawn on brown paper "to provide a softer, more literal image that the congregation would respond to."[12]

Lundy also produced the presentation drawings for Lucaya, an unbuilt 1973 resort project for Bradenton, Florida, using the combination of Wolff's Carbon Pencils for the detailed work and charcoal for the looser elements that Lundy favored, but he did them on drafting film, in the manner of labeled and numbered working drawings[13] (fig. 12). He would use the same media to achieve a very different effect in his much later rendering of the sanctuary of St. Paul's Lutheran Church in Sarasota (fig. 1, page 28). But here they were loose and watery, well suited for a harbor basin framed by swaying palms, with sinuous island-tipped boat slips cast like a necklace on its waters. By 1969 Lundy had further developed this presentation technique, using mixed media on drafting film to represent his designs for a parking structure for the State University of New York at Cortland (fig. 11). Lundy remains very proud of his concept for this parking garage, which solved a special problem, where "arrival was at a much lower level and the parking structure kept unfolding deeper and upward until you exited at the campus level above," and selected this special technique to showcase his design. The trees are charcoal, as are the water and grass. In 1970 he employed this same technique to good effect in a conjectural rendering meant to demonstrate to the administrators of what was then the Smithsonian Institution's Museum of History and Technology that his 1965 shade structures for that building's terraces could be reused over a hypothetical, terraced Pre-Columbian exhibition[14] (fig. 13).

Lundy also exhibited proficiency in producing more traditional presentation drawings, as is evident in his 1997 perspective rendering for the Hagler Foundation, the private fund-raising entity for Texas A&M University in College Station, Texas (fig. 14). Lundy's subtly toned washes, all done by hand over lightly drawn graphite outlines, bring the elegant forms of the curving, barrel-vaulted colonnade of his neoclassical scheme for this project to life, through his complete understanding and mastery of light and shadow. Under the Beaux-Arts system all architects were trained as students to be able to produce such seductive ink-and-wash perspectives, at first as part of their student exams and competitions, and later to show and to sell projects to their clients. But since World War II relatively few professional architects have been taught such skills. Most contemporary architectural firms usually either engage a professional architectural illustrator or, if large enough, have a specialist on the staff for this purpose, often a person who also employs computer-assisted drafting (CAD) and digital illustration software. Architects with artistic mastery such as Lundy's are rare.

For an exhibition of his and his wife's work shown in Marfa, Texas, in 2006, Lundy, then in his eighties, produced a remarkable retrospective series of large-scale perspective renderings of selected examples of his earlier work… a daunting task for an artist of any age.[15] To represent the sanctuary that he originally designed in 1969 for St. Paul's Lutheran Church, he produced a stunning eight-by-four-foot rendering in carbon pencil and charcoal on heavy paper.[16] In a vision both calm and luminous, even ethereal, Lundy the artist poetically conveyed the original intentions that Lundy the architect conceived for this structure and space.[17] The drawing also serves as an eloquent argument that subsequent adornments added by the congregation compromise the purity of his design.

All of Lundy's presentation drawings were of course preceded by sketches and preliminary drawings in which Lundy developed ideas that the final works embodied. Thousands are to be found in what Lundy called his "brains books," bound notebooks like those used by students, roughly eight by ten inches, but extraordinary in that their thousands of pages contain much more than just sketches. Drawings appear in the context of thousands of pages of supplemental information, ranging from Lundy's notes on sites, concepts, clients, projects, materials, construction, and budgets to personal sketches, notes, thoughts, and observations relating to all aspects of his life, travels, family, friends, colleagues, and acquaintances. They concern his

Fig. 24 Detail of Corinthian capital on the Pantheon, Rome, from Lundy's travel sketchbook, 1948–1950. Watercolor and graphite on paper, 20 x 24 inches

many passions, including the natural and built environments, art, nature, music, and much more. They are enriched further by Lundy's observant recordings and reactions to the work, lectures, and presentations of many of the leading architects, engineers, critics, and historians of his time. They constitute a unique record of American and international architecture and life over almost half a century (from 1959 until 2009), and promise to be a rich and continuing resource for students and researchers in many disciplines.

A few examples demonstrate the uniqueness of his insights. In developing his design for the First Unitarian Congregational Society of Hartford, Connecticut, in 1961 Lundy began by examining the nature and liturgy of Unitarianism itself, including the relationship of the congregation to the minister and how those things shaped their spatial needs. One page of an associated brains book includes a sketch of a traditional church interior with the minister in his pulpit surrounded by Lundy's initial observations:

> All the things that man has & sees is intrinsically "one"
> Look inward—plunge into the depths of his own personality
> *introverted* consciousness…
>
> *Changing levels, changing approaches leads to a unity*
> *which is the starting point* *

Similarly, in 1965 for the US Tax Court Building in Washington, DC, Lundy sketched on two adjoining pages the forms of a traditional American courthouse with a central monumental dome, portico, and broad flight of stairs flanked by lower wings, commenting: "Make an event of it" (fig. 15). Next he sketched alternative elevations and plans echoing that tripartite formula in a more modern monumental idiom, retaining the divisions and the idea of a broad, monumental staircase: "Judges at 1 end—courts in between.... Make more complicated—simple serene—and good taste—nice—looks like a court House [not an] office building."[18]

In another book from 1965, in notes by Lundy on what he recalls as a rather stodgy lecture, "Structural Innovations in Masonry," he produced a series of imaginative and energetic sketches expressing his "completely opposite reaction" to what was being presented[19] (fig. 16). They are not dissimilar to the sophisticated computer-assisted forms of the architect Greg Lynn's 1999 *Embryological House*.[20] Lundy's notes state the goals for which he was striving in those sketches: "A total serene form—A tension of brick and wood—Simple form—tie in with great sweeping lines of earth sculpture. Simple serene planes of material."

A 1961 brains book includes several pages on Lundy's design for the competition for a memorial to President Franklin D. Roosevelt. A single page succinctly encapsulates his analysis of the essential elements of the Lincoln and Jefferson memorials and his complementary transformation of their forms into a new one where columns become the radial arms of a flowerlike bowl, itself an inverted dome with a sculpture at its center.

A particular attribute of these journals is their extensive documentation of the site and its attributes and of the architect's dialogue with the same in his efforts to develop appropriate functional and expressive forms for a project. This process often was a paramount concern for Lundy, as can be seen in a 1959 notebook, one of his first, for a resort building for the Sierra Blanca Ski Resort in Ruidoso, New Mexico. His respect for and appreciation of the landscape, and his recognition of its potential, is the source for an original and innovative design that rests carefully on the site without erasing its features. Rather, it recognizes and emphasizes them. These concerns are evident in both his sketch and his notes: "open fretwork of piers—Sense of land floating under. Sense of water meandering under bldg."

Whether large or small, the site can be the most critical element in a plan. In 1966 Lundy devoted many pages in several brains books to his study and analysis of the site of a proposed beach house for Mr. and Mrs. Ben Heller at East Hampton, Long Island (unbuilt). These pages demonstrate Lundy's talents as both architect and artist. His aerial perspective dated July 25, 1966, shows the "tangled" roof forms of the house complementing the neighboring dunes, with the following description (fig. 17):

> Like the dunes—a simple yet complicated timeless sculptural house of cedar shingles where sweeping roofs hang & tangle naturally over a plan that works—over rooms that face the right way and function naturally and beautifully on this magnificent site. Like the old great houses with shaggy thick shingled silhouettes, but not heavy like them. A timeless house of today and tomorrow of this century—natural, easy, simple, rugged. One and at home with the dunes & the sea—yet endless, interesting—with an endless variety.

Lundy the artist is seen in the accompanying two-page color sketch, an impressionistic portrait of the dunes, with one of

Long Island's distinctive windmills tucked into its background (fig. 18).

After the grand tour provided by the Rotch Scholarship in the late 1940s, Lundy continued to produce travel sketches throughout his career, and these constitute one of the most significant aspects of his artistic legacy. Often stunning in their beauty and highly original in their point of view and use of media, they are worthy of a study of their own. In addition to his traditional graphite, ink, and watercolor sketches and renderings, Lundy readily employed newer media, including colored markers and oil pastels.[21] The use of both of the latter is evident in his dramatic and highly inventive view of the courtyard of Prague Castle, which he framed looking through the entrance of the iconic Bull Staircase designed by the distinguished Slovenian architect Jože Plečnik (fig. 19). The colored markers provided a shortcut, which allowed Lundy to do the drawing within a constricted time frame.[22]

In Rome Lundy favored a number of subjects that he drew many times.[23] One was the famous Trevi Fountain, which for him was a subject of abstracted curvilinear and jagged forms, intense color, and light and shadow, with glistening white marble silhouetted against a dark background (fig. 20). Also using oil pastels, but in two tones rather than in many hues, he rendered the dramatically curving baroque cornice of the main facade of Francesco Borromini's church of San Carlo alle Quattro Fontane, from an equally unusual point of view—vertiginous, almost worm's-eye, and close-up (fig. 21).

On the other side of the world, in Mexico, in the 1970s Lundy filled another large sketchbook with images of buildings and sites in Oaxaca and Nochistlán and their vicinity. The urban spaces of both are captured in his richly colored, double-page oil pastel portraits of the church and former monastery of Santo Domingo de Guzmán in Oaxaca and the plaza and fountain of Nochistlán (fig. 22). The view of Oaxaca is flat, its elevation almost like a stage set, while his deep-perspective view of Nochistlán employs the Renaissance perspective principles of foreground, middle ground, and background to great effect. The facade of an unidentified church in a sketchbook from this trip is shown at an angle, framed like a jewel by light stucco walls, the elaborate sculptural decoration and rich colors of its baroque facade blending together as Lundy took advantage of the fact that his oil pastels were melting in the intense heat[24] (fig. 23).

Lundy's oil pastel travel sketches, however beautiful, lacked the extra precision afforded by graphite and watercolor, and his decades of experience and mastery of watercolor rendering as both architect and artist are evident in one of this author's favorite examples of his work. Among his multiple studies of the Roman Pantheon, a watercolor close-up of the details of one of its Corinthian capitals distills the essence of Mediterranean sunlight caressing the voluptuous organic forms of its acanthus leaves and volutes in a dramatic play of light, shadow, and liquid washes[25] (fig. 24).

Lundy's work is exceptional in many ways. It is distinguished by its intelligence, its variety, its skill, and its humanity. It is filled with the energy of a prodigious imagination fueled by unbounded curiosity and a keenly sensitive eye. Moreover, it is imbued with a palpable sense of joy and wonder about the experience and observation of the real world, and about how both art and architecture can serve as invaluable tools to advance an individual's and society's enjoyment, appreciation, understanding, and even improvement of that world.

The Sarasota Years

Christopher S. Wilson

In the 1950s, Florida's temperate weather, natural beauty, and laid-back lifestyle attracted families to move and live there year-round.[1] Sarasota in particular attracted writers, painters, photographers, musicians, and architects, its artistic atmosphere and cultural reputation having been first established in the 1930s by the circus magnate John Ringling and his Ringling Museum and Ringling School of Art.[2] In 1953 the director of New York's Metropolitan Museum of Art, Francis Taylor, proclaimed that there was no place in the entire southeastern United States that possessed such a wealth of art and wonderful surroundings as Sarasota.[3]

As a result of this environment, Sarasota was generally friendlier than other parts of the country to new ideas and artistic practices—particularly modern architecture. The "Sarasota School of Architecture"—better described as a movement—was a regional variation of modern architecture that thrived in Sarasota and southwest Florida between 1940 and 1970.[4] Architects took their aesthetic cues from the modern architecture that had developed during the 1920s and 1930s in Europe—geometric volumes, flat roofs, lack of applied decoration, limited color palette—but adapted those forms to the Florida climate, where the extremes of sunshine and rain could be controlled to provide year-round outdoor living. The architects Ralph Twitchell

(1890–1978) and Paul Rudolph (1918–1997) are credited with starting the Sarasota School just before World War II. Tim Seibert, Mark Hampton, Gene Leedy, Jack West, William Rupp, Bert Brosmith, Joseph Farrell, Frank Folsom Smith, Carl Abbott, and Victor Lundy were also prominent members. In an era like today's, when "sustainability" and environmentally friendly practices are held in high esteem, much can be learned from Sarasota School characteristics such as large, overhanging eaves that provide shading to glass walls, single-room depths that allow for natural ventilation, and a close relationship between inside and outside.

Lundy lived and worked in Sarasota from 1952 to 1960, although his office there did not officially close until 1963. Lundy's initial exposure to the area came through his partnership with fellow Harvard Graduate School of Design (GSD) graduate Reginald Caywood Knight (1921–1973), which lasted from about 1950 to 1954. Knight and Lundy's projects were mostly private residences for illustrators associated with the Famous Artists School, a correspondence course founded in 1948 in Westport, Connecticut, by Norman Rockwell and eleven other commercial artists.[5]

One of those founding artists, Ben Stahl, had been wintering since 1939 in Sarasota, and in 1951 commissioned a house from Knight and Lundy to serve as his year-round

Fig. 1 Frontenac Hotel, Lido Key, Sarasota, Florida, 1959

Fig. 2 Stahl House, Ben Stahl and family in their glass-walled living room, Sarasota, Florida, 1955

residence. The Stahl House was made of reinforced concrete beams forming a grid of sixteen rectangles, which, because they were supported on only twelve columns, produced many two-way cantilevers (fig. 2). Because of Knight and Lundy's modernist architectural education from the GSD (run at that time by Bauhaus founder Walter Gropius), all the walls consisted of floor-to-ceiling glass. Stahl later commented, "We were like goldfish in a bowl....They knew I was a painter, that I would have pictures to hang on the walls [but] that place had no walls to hang a picture on."[6] Possibly disillusioned with this and previous experiences with Knight of making purely formalist modernist architecture, Lundy dissolved their partnership during the construction of the Stahl House.[7]

After the termination of their partnership, both architects stayed in Florida. Knight designed several more buildings in Sarasota, as well as civic, commercial, educational, and religious buildings elsewhere in the state, before moving to New York City in the mid-1960s.[8] Lundy also stayed in the area because, in his own words, "What I rejoiced in was... working hard, swimming in the Gulf [of Mexico], and being renewed everyday...[in this] wonderful place."[9]

After separating from Knight, Lundy's first project was a church for the Presbyterian Congregation of Venice/Nokomis in southern Sarasota County (fig. 3). Completed in 1954, this building is also known as the "drive-in church" because congregants would park their cars in front of the structure and, like at a drive-in movie, remain in them while listening

to the church service on speakers attached to their windows. Set on an 8.5-acre site among native pine trees, the building itself was a two-story, wood-and-glass podium containing the minister's pulpit, organist, and choir on the upper story, and a Sunday School and office space on the ground floor.[10] The shed roof of the building angles upward in the direction of the cars, perhaps to express the direction of communication from minister to congregation, and foreshadowed Lundy's more dramatic structures to come. The angle was heightened by the tapering of the roof beams from their full depth at the column supports to a minimal dimension at their ends.

Two other projects from 1954, one built and one unbuilt, also contain a slightly up-tilted roof with beams tapered at their ends. The built work was a residence for Mr. and Mrs. Harry Berk in the Forest Lakes subdivision of Sarasota, a modest, one-story, open-plan suburban residence with attached garage. The unbuilt work was a proposal for Mr. Berk's Pure Ice Company for a small building containing an automated ice dispenser.[11]

The story behind the commissioning of Lundy's next built work, for the Sarasota Chamber of Commerce, illustrates his often-spoken statement that "my art form—all my life— has been architecture."[12] In 1955 Lundy entered a watercolor into the annual Sarasota Art Fair and was awarded Best of Show. Karl Bickel, a prominent local citizen and member of the Chamber of Commerce Building Committee, saw this

Fig. 3 Church for the Presbyterian Congregation of Venice/Nokomis (the "drive-in church"), Venice, Florida, 1954

Fig. 4 Sarasota County Chamber of Commerce Building, Sarasota, Florida, 1955. Casein painting on paper
Fig. 5 (opposite) Sarasota County Chamber of Commerce Building, Sarasota, Florida, 1956
Fig. 6 (following spread) Sarasota County Chamber of Commerce Building, Sarasota, Florida, 1956

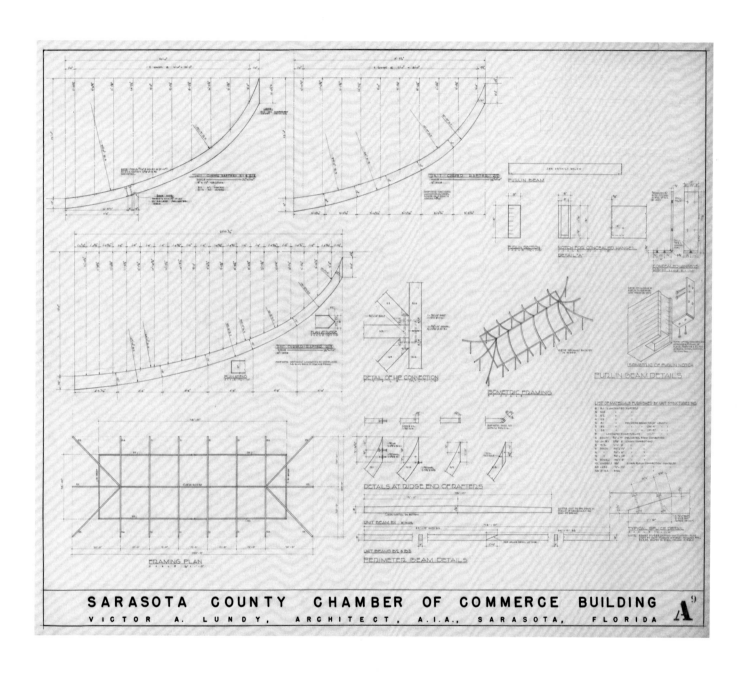

Fig. 7 Sarasota County Chamber of Commerce Building, roof-framing materials and wood details, drawing A9, 1955

artwork and prize and asked Lundy for a building proposal.[13] Instead of a typical architect's sketch, Lundy painted a series of large casein-based paintings showing an Asian-styled pavilion and was subsequently awarded the commission (fig. 4).

Nicknamed "The Pagoda Building" (or "The Blue Pagoda"), the Sarasota Chamber of Commerce was completed in 1956. It is a low-lying horizontal structure, thirty by eighty feet, with a curvaceously hipped roof. Because of the full-height glass sides, the roof seems to float above the ground. The visual heaviness of this roof, with its blue tiles, adds to the magic of the illusion.[14] The building's unique roof shape is constructed from curved laminated timber beams that are supported on steel columns. Impressively, within a limited budget of only $50,000, Lundy also air-conditioned the building by running ducts in the floor, leaving the roof beams exposed and unobstructed (figs. 5–7).

The Sarasota Chamber of Commerce marked a turning point in Lundy's career. First, it solidified his entry into the Sarasota architectural scene, which until then had been dominated by Rudolph. From that point onward, there would be a tacit competition in town between the two figures, although, in reality, their modes of expression and methods of working were completely different.[15] It also marked the emergence of a more distinctive style of work: after the Sarasota Chamber of Commerce, laminated-timber roof beams became a hallmark of Lundy's work, particularly in his churches. Bee Ridge Presbyterian Church and a more traditional replacement of the drive-in church (which was demolished) for the Presbyterian Congregation of Venice/Nokomis soon followed, both completed in 1956, and both using laminated-timber roof beams. Speaking at the "Design and Aesthetics in Wood" conference in 1967, Lundy remarked on the use of wood in architecture, particularly modern architecture:

> Wood is a living, resilient material. It is totally unlike steel or concrete. It has air in it. It comes mainly from above the earth, not beneath the earth....As a material, it should be a modern medium of construction. It should be given as much consideration as a contemporary construction medium as steel or concrete. New techniques can make it go beyond the limits of tree sizes, tree strengths and natural fire resistance.[16]

Lundy's next project was a clubhouse for the Colony Beach Club on Longboat Key, one of the barrier islands off the coast of Sarasota[17] (fig. 8). The club was founded in 1954 by Herbert Field as a tourist resort consisting of 110 single-story cottages.[18] Lundy's clubhouse, located directly on the beach in the center of the complex, served as a common space where guests could meet and dine. The shape of Lundy's design was a little over a quarter segment of a circle, with the concave side facing the water. The structure consisted of a simple grid of wooden columns and beams with walls of full-height glass. The clubhouse for the Colony Beach Club, along with the Sarasota Chamber of Commerce, Bee Ridge, and the Venice/Nokomis Presbyterian churches, was a sure indication that Lundy, while still a modernist, would not be following in the strict geometric footsteps of his Harvard GSD education.

In 1955 Lundy befriended Rolland King and Frank Smith, described in the June 1957 issue of *Architectural Forum* as "young Sarasota developers who fly their own black-and-gold company plane."[19] Two projects from this acquaintance were eventually constructed: an office building for King & Smith on Siesta Drive and a community center and pool complex for their South Gate subdivision in Sarasota. Both buildings were completed in 1956. The office building uses steel trusses in its sloped-wing roof. Alternating solid walls of brick and granite stop at seven feet and are continued with clerestory glass, allowing both natural light and privacy. Non-load-bearing internal partitions were made to be moved as needed.[20] Lundy's South Gate Community Center consists of two parts: a rectilinear assembly hall with glass walls and straight, laminated-timber roof beams making an uncharacteristically flat roof, and a segmented, circular-shaped building containing support spaces for the pool. Two of the four walls of the assembly hall are full-height, twelve-foot glass, allowing clear views out to the Phillippi Creek. The walls of the curved building are composed of undulating masonry units, making an interesting and inexpensive wall texture.

During 1957 Lundy completed one commercial structure, one civic structure, and several residences. At first glance, the Joe Barth Insurance Company Building seems atypical for Lundy because of its simple, rectangular, glass-and-steel box structure. Upon further examination, the building reveals an ingenious subtlety: its structural grid is rotated forty-five degrees relative to the street, resulting in a dynamic zigzag facade, giving an expressive twist to a modernist rational box.[21] The Tourist Center for Silver Springs, Florida—a state park built around a group of

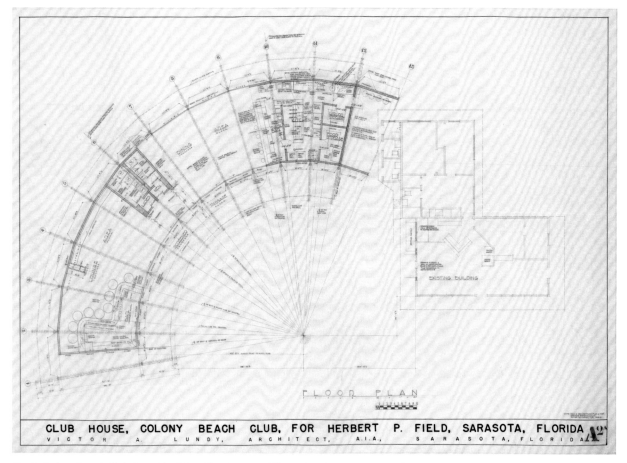

CLUB HOUSE, COLONY BEACH CLUB, FOR HERBERT P. FIELD, SARASOTA, FLORIDA
VICTOR A. LUNDY, ARCHITECT, A.I.A., SARASOTA, FLORIDA

Fig. 8 Colony Beach Club, Long Boat Key, Florida, revised floor plan, drawing 2A, October 25, 1956
Fig. 9 (opposite) Dudley Residence, Siesta Key, Sarasota, Florida, 1957
Fig. 10 (following spread) Herron House, Venice, Florida, 1957, photographed in 2017

artesian springs—consists of two curving, parallel structures. The first, directly on the Silver River, is a covered walkway providing sun and rain shelter for a tourist boat dock. The second curving building contains shops, restrooms, and offices. The entire project is framed in steel, with all columns and beams exposed. As is typical of Lundy projects, vertical walls do not reach the roof; instead, there is clerestory glass above them, making the roof appear to float.

As compared with Lundy's Sarasota peers, whose main commissions were residential, he completed only five houses during his time in Sarasota. Three were built in 1957: the Eareckson Residence on Siesta Key (another of Sarasota's barrier islands), the Dudley Residence in the Sandy Hook development (also on Siesta Key), and the Herron Residence, in the southern Sarasota County town of Venice.

The Eareckson Residence was designed for the family of Colonel William Eareckson (1900–1966). The house consists of a centralized, high-ceilinged living room, overlooking Sarasota Bay, surrounded by one-story volumes containing the kitchen and children's bedrooms. A master suite is above the living room, with the same view. The folded-plate roofs zigzag up and down, and are supported on exposed wooden beams and columns. Lundy also designed a matching wooden boathouse with an undulating roof. The Dudley Residence was designed for the family of retired business executive Joseph D. Dudley (1904–1975). Mrs. Dudley was a painter, for whom Lundy provided a special room. This $30,000 house, a wooden space frame built up from standard timber sizes, has masonry, glass, and screen walls as in-fill. An expressive wood-and-screen, prow-like structure grows out of the west side of the main house, providing a screened-in children's play space on the ground floor and balcony on the upper floor. The balcony actually extends the entire west side of the house but is only screened-in at the

Fig. 11 (previous spread) Herron House, Venice, Florida, 1957, photographed in 2017
Fig. 12 Herron House, Venice, Florida, 1957

prow, resulting in an interesting spatial complexity. The construction details of this house are notable for their inexpensive yet effective visual tactics: on the ground floor, the mortar of the masonry walls purposely oozes out of the walls' joints to create a visual texture, and upstairs the vertical wood strips of the wood paneling are not spaced equally, providing an interesting irregular rhythm to otherwise ordinary walls (fig. 9).

Lundy's final house of 1957 is perhaps his best. The Herron House, built for a real estate developer and fellow World War II veteran, Samuel H. Herron (1922–2005), is series of masonry cubes arranged around a cylindrical central living room, all beneath an overarching roof composed of laminated, W-shaped timber beams. The ends are cantilevered, making the house look like a bird in flight. In this building, too, the masonry walls stop short of the roof at about seven feet, and clerestory windows fill the vertical surface up to the ceiling. A separate cylindrical garage composed of undulating masonry units completes the playfulness of the main house[22] (figs. 10–12).

Beginning in 1958, Lundy's expressionistic tendencies began to take on metaphorical and particularly organic characteristics. An addition to the Alta Vista Elementary School provided six classrooms on either side of a skylit corridor by means of laminated-timber beams spaced fourteen feet apart. Like the Herron House, these beams are shaped like a W. An eighteen-foot cantilever on either side provides shaded outdoor classroom space, giving the nickname "butterfly wings" to these overhangs. While the budget for Alta Vista was still modest for its size ($154,000 for about 10,000 square feet), from this point onward Lundy's projects and budgets were beginning to increase in both scale and scope (figs. 13–17).

The Warm Mineral Springs Motel, also completed in 1958, is in North Port, a town in southern Sarasota County. Standing at the entrance road to the Warm Mineral Springs—a natural sinkhole, deep-vent spring touted as Ponce de León's "fountain of youth"—this motel, although not officially associated with the springs, was developed privately to meet the needs of those who stayed for several

ADDITION TO THE ALTA VISTA ELEMENTARY SCHOOL, SARASOTA, FLORIDA

Fig. 13 Addition to the Alta Vista Elementary School, Sarasota, Florida, rendering, 1956
Fig. 14 Addition to the Alta Vista Elementary School, Sarasota, Florida, 1958
Fig. 15 (following spread) Addition to the Alta Vista Elementary School, Sarasota, Florida, 1958

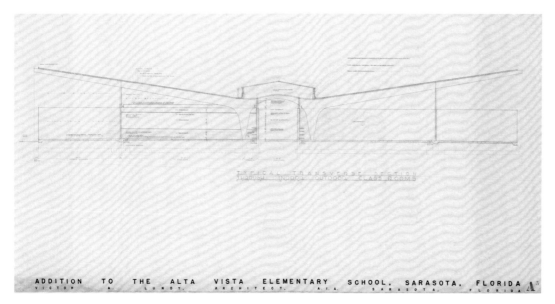

ADDITION TO THE ALTA VISTA ELEMENTARY SCHOOL, SARASOTA, FLORIDA
VICTOR A. LUNDY, ARCHITECT, A.I.A. SARASOTA, FLORIDA

Fig. 16 Addition to the Alta Vista Elementary School, Sarasota, Florida, section, ca. 1957
Fig. 17 Addition to the Alta Vista Elementary School, Sarasota, Florida, 1958

days or more, swimming in the mineral-rich waters for restorative health purposes. The building consists of what Lundy has called a "forest of architectural palms": seventy-five 8-inch, precast concrete columns topped with mushroom-like hyperbolic paraboloids—precast concrete, 14.5 by 14.5 feet by 2 inches thick, arranged at two different levels in a checker-board pattern. The vertical space between the upper and lower paraboloids is filled in with acrylic sheeting.[23] The motel was originally L-shaped, but was later extended into a U. The walls facing the courtyard are full-height glass, while the walls facing the parking lot are made out of undulating masonry units stopping at door level to make clerestory windows. Like previous Lundy projects, air conditioning ducts run under the floor slab to each room in order not to disturb the aesthetics of the roof structure. A road sign with three "mushroom" columns and playful, cursive typography acted to attract drivers' attention and entice them to stay, even if they would not be visiting the springs (figs. 18–20).

By 1959 Lundy solidified his organic metaphor design sensibility with the Galloway's Furniture Showroom, one of seven branches of the store headquartered in Tampa, run by Ralph Galloway (1916–2002). In the text for Lundy's 1961 AIA Honor Awards submission, he described the building as follows:

> A "morning glory" shape of laminated redwood arches, the building is a potent company symbol. Like the stems of a symmetrical plant, 16 laminated redwood bents curve outward from a central base to support the roof of the glass-walled structure.

Located on the heavily trafficked Tamiami Trail just south of downtown Sarasota, the cylindrical glass-walled building was intended to draw the attention of passersby, especially at night when, along with its gold-anodized glass framing, it appeared to glow. The laminated roof timbers curved down to a central area housing mechanical and restroom spaces, making the entire floor plan free to exhibit the furniture, which would then be ordered directly from Tampa (no storage necessary). The roof is constructed from Douglas fir decking on top of the laminated timbers, with a finished ceiling surface of redwood. A mezzanine was hung from the roof structure, and a stair was hung from that. The mezza-nine broke up the large height of the space, giving the

showroom a more residential feel appropriate for the living room and bedroom displays. Similarly, the sample fixtures provided all lighting in the showroom. Again, air-conditioning was provided in the floor so as not to interrupt the roof structure. Holes were cut in the overhanging roof to save two existing Australian pine trees. Lundy cleverly located the building's two entrances at the location of these trees and roof holes. The ultimate success of this showroom came from Lundy's ability to combine his artistic design intentions with Galloway's business objectives to produce a one-of-a-kind commercial space[24] (figs. 21–26).

That year, Lundy completed his final residence in Sarasota, the Elvgren Residence on Siesta Key, for the family of Gil Elvgren (1914–1980), a famous illustrator best known for his pinup posters. The house plan—a central living/dining/kitchen area parallel to the Sarasota Bay with angled bedroom wings—was a product of the clients' desire to make the most of their waterfront property, ensuring that each area of the house had a view and received breezes. The wooden beams and columns, built up from standard sizes, were all carefully articulated and exposed. To brighten the living area sheltered by wide porch overhangs, the roof beams extend up along the inland-facing side to form a continuous clerestory. Exterior masonry walls were composed of a buff-colored concrete block, stacked vertically, and the fireplace wall—similar to the Eareckson Residence—was made from local coquina stone. The mantelpiece of this structure interestingly extends out horizontally through a full-height window into the screened porch.[25] Lundy's opinion of this $50,000 house was that "it is an informal house and one feels about it that little chil-dren, dogs, and parakeets are welcome, as well as people."[26]

In 1959 Lundy completed the thirty-two-room Frontenac Hotel on Lido Key, another of Sarasota's barrier islands. This beach accommodation is a simple rectilinear concrete frame with three expressive elements: one vertical, one horizontal, and one spiral. The vertical concrete elements were precast and prestressed and marked the hotel's entry as a sculptural composition. The horizontal elements were cantilevered, precast- and prestressed-concrete and provided a second floor and roof, their ends forming a scalloped edge. The second-floor handrail and the ground floor level paving also follow this scalloped pattern in the vertical dimension. The spiral elements were concrete stairs on each end of the building (fig. 1, page 52, and figs. 27–28).

(continued on page 85)

Fig. 18 Warm Mineral Springs Inn, North Port, Florida, 1958

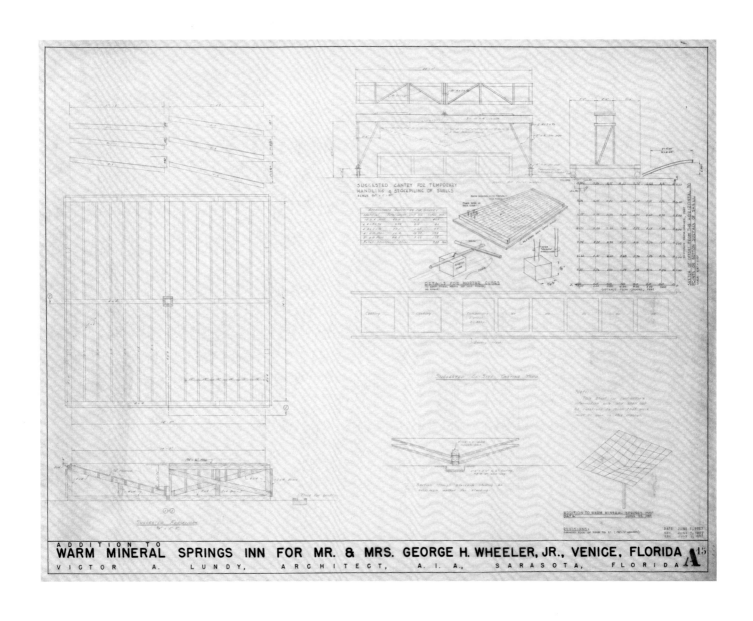

Fig. 19 (above) Warm Mineral Springs Inn, North Port, Florida, details for on-site casting, drawing A15, dated July 1, 1957

Fig. 20 (following spread) Warm Mineral Springs Inn, North Port, Florida, exterior with view into rooms, 1958

Fig. 21 Galloway's Furniture Showroom, Sarasota, Florida, 1959. Pencil sketch of interior on tracing paper

Fig. 22 Galloway's Furniture Showroom, Sarasota, Florida, 1959. Pencil sketch of exterior on tracing paper
Fig. 23 (opposite) Galloway's Furniture Showroom, Sarasota, Florida, roof detail, 1959

In 1960 Lundy also moved his residence to Guilford, Connecticut, and opened an office in New York City.[27] One employee, Boyd Blackner, stayed behind in Sarasota to complete jobs in progress—mostly churches to be discussed in the next chapter—and eventually to close the office in 1963.[28] There are three unbuilt projects from this time that are worth mentioning, as they foreshadow Lundy's post-Sarasota career. First, following the commercial success of Galloway's Furniture Showroom, Mr. and Mrs. Galloway began discussions with Lundy about a residence in Tampa. Lundy met with the Galloways on many occasions and took substantial notes in his "brains books" about their aesthetic preferences and design philosophies. The comment that perhaps best summarizes Lundy's thinking at this time was, "How we do it is what makes us artists. It is familiar and strange all at once. Logic—that which makes the familiar strange and the strange familiar."[29] Throughout the rest of his career, Lundy's architectural practice was a constant search for new ideas and forms, rather than the repetition of successful past projects. The second unbuilt project, a simple sketch for a bubble-shaped building to house the Sarasota Ballet, is variously described by Lundy as a parasol, umbrella, seashell, cocoon, parachute, tent, and the ruffled skirt of a ballet dancer. Here, Lundy pushed his metaphorical design method to the extreme.[30] Lastly, a more finalized but also unbuilt project was a community center for the Sarasota Mobile Home Park. Lundy's detailed section and floor plans reveal a massive 127-foot-diameter building with a further 20-foot, all-around overhang. This proposal was the next logical step after Galloway's Furniture Showroom in terms of scale and vocabulary and, had it been built, would have overshadowed all of Lundy's previous Sarasota projects.[31]

The fertile and creative atmosphere of 1950s Sarasota, with its enlightened clients, healthy competition, and pleasant climate, also provided Victor Lundy with the inspiration and drive to move away from his rational and geometric education at Harvard to a more individual expression, which he continued to develop through the rest of his career. Lundy's architecture, especially in Sarasota, is better known for its rooflines—sometimes described as "more roof than wall."[32] Lundy himself has characterized his architecture as having "strong, easily recognized images, because [he tries] to make architecture say something boldly, clearly, simply."[34] This idea remains apparent in the buildings he designed after he left Sarasota.

Fig. 24 (previous spread, left) Galloway's Furniture Showroom, Sarasota, Florida, 1959
Fig. 25 (previous spread, right) Galloway's Furniture Showroom, Sarasota, Florida, ceiling detail, 1959
Fig. 26 Galloway's Furniture Showroom, Sarasota, Florida, interior stair, 1959

Fig. 27 (opposite) Frontenac Hotel, Lido Key, Sarasota, Florida, 1959
Fig. 28 (above) Frontenac Hotel, Lido Key, Sarasota, Florida, 1959

Sacred Spaces

Christopher Domin

The landscape along the west coast of Florida must have seemed like a contemporary Eden to someone like Victor Lundy, who spent his childhood in Manhattan. With miles of undeveloped shoreline and acres of pine forest, this region's primal character attracted many postwar transplants. With a rapidly growing population, it also provided the perfect backdrop for Lundy's early church designs, in particular his first, designed for the Venice/Nokomis Presbyterian congregation in Venice, Florida—what became known as the drive-in church. The small Presbyterian congregation had seen Lundy's artwork published in the newspaper and met with Lundy to discuss his unusual building idea: to convert the site of a former drive-in theater into a place of worship.[1] In Lundy's aerial rendering, the natural beauty and vast open space of the site gracefully upstages the architecture. With nature as the backdrop and a minimal steel cross reaching for the sky, the site is convincingly transformed toward the sacred (fig. 1). With its lucid expression of local wood technology, the pulpit pavilion honors the structural determinism of Walter Gropius and his former Bauhaus colleagues, but the raised platform in the trees that Lundy devised is also imbued with a sense of surprise. Allowing for an abundance of pine forest surrounding the pulpit where nature and religion align, a new order is established,

signaling the freedom of expression and lack of constraint that was endemic in this outpost along the west coast of Florida at the time.

Set on a level site punctuated with groupings of established trees, informal clusters of cars and open-air seating mingle with the diminutive built structure. At first glance, this work more resembles a campsite than a traditional church or chapel. The building is a small part of the larger landscape. Interior and exterior spaces merge in the composition, the built spaces deferring and opening up to the vast landscape and benevolent climate.[2] Describing his creative process for this project, Lundy writes:

> I find an answer sometimes in almost reverting to a naive, childlike approach—of purposely not paying attention to what others are doing—of treating each problem as if it were the first—of trying to get to the fundamentals—the essence of architecture. Like being alone with only a forest of trees and your hands, and having the problem of building a shelter.[3]

For Lundy, meaningfully situated architecture found its reason for being in the intimate details of the region and the essence of the materials employed. Lundy's post and beam

Fig. 1 Church for the Presbyterian Congregation of Venice/Nokomis, (the "drive-in church"), Venice, Florida, view of pulpit, 1954

speaker's platform echoed the slender trunks of the neighboring pine trees. The structural clarity of natural elements, including the spatial ordering of the longleaf pine ecosystem with its dappled canopy of light, must have resonated with an architect who was searching for an essential condition in architectural expression. In practice, outdoor work and life was already a part of the local culture, making its way into the design of schools, residences, and public buildings through the use of courtyards, shade structures, and large sliding walls of glass. A primary question for Lundy, in these early constructions, may have been—how little does one have to build to meet basic programmatic requirements? For the Venice/Nokomis Presbyterian congregation, Lundy found that the economy and directness of this way of building and the access it provided to nature suited the daily needs of his client.

It was in Lundy's next two projects, a Fellowship Hall for the Venice/Nokomis Presbyterian congregation and a sanctuary at the Bee Ridge Church in Sarasota, where the work evolved (figs. 2–4). In these projects, glue-laminated timbers form a woven system of pointed arches, with masonry firmly anchoring the space to the ground. Under these sheltering enclosures, earth and sky are linked in these places of worship with their outward connections to the surrounding landscape. Their strong foundational walls and relatively light vaulted wood roofs provide the congregation with a devotional room that is intimately scaled, but clearly separate from spaces of daily life.[4] During this period, Lundy's distinctly articulated volumes and his interest in materiality are a departure from the increasingly banal conception of universal space embraced by many architects in his generation. Strategically leveraging material qualities, texture, and color in the work helped Lundy situate his idea of space within a larger historical continuum and provide a sense of scale. His response to the specific needs of each situation allowed for a unique integration of architecture, structure, and light that held the aspirations of client, architect, and community alike. In this early group of buildings from the first decade of his practice, formal legibility became an important characteristic of Lundy's work:

> My buildings tend to have a strong, easily recognized image because I try to make architecture say something boldly, clearly, simply. The great ideas in art are not covered over with complicated layers of intellectualism. If one is too conscious of the clever workings of the complex creative mind he may lose sight of what he is meant to see. The great artists are primitives, and what they say touches on fundamental ideas common to many men.[5]

In another context, Lundy described his work as "one shot out of structure" and this embrace of structural expressionism is also a primary strategy of resistance to the increasingly homogenized suburban landscape and suited Lundy's developing specialty in the design of sacred space.[6]

Before Lundy had a body of built work to share with potential clients, he used original drawings, made during his travels, of churches and other places of worship to assist in explaining his design principles and to place the development of a new project within a long lineage of sacred building typology. Unlike many of his colleagues, Lundy did not have an inherent distrust of historical investigation or even overt and enthusiastic references to the past in his published essays and built work. The spatial and structural logic of Gothic, baroque, or even early Christian architecture are part of his frame of reference and provide a point of departure that often set Lundy apart from his generational cohort.

His built work exudes a sophisticated knowledge of light and material (fig. 5). Shadow and matter merge to form spaces that feel simultaneously archaic and also rooted in contemporary culture. For Lundy, the outward character of his creations began to take on a symbolic function, as well: "We need symbols in architecture; we need them especially in church architecture. A church should look like a church, inside and out, and when it does, it becomes a symbol. It must look and be what it is without further explanation."[7]

In Lundy's mind, there was always a dialogue between the individual and the communal. While "the design of the place of worship is a crystallization, a concentration in one ultimate statement," Lundy also knew that these spaces must respond to the daily needs of a diverse population. He wrote:

> People differ greatly in what they require and in what they want in a place of worship. Some need tradition, or certain elements of it. The designer of the church building cannot turn his back on the past, for history and the church and people are not separable: the past is the heritage of faith, and a people's desire to see this expressed is right.
>
> Because the place of worship is a place for people, its qualities, however expressed, must be fundamental,

Fig. 2 (previous page) Bee Ridge Presbyterian Church, Sarasota, Florida, sanctuary before completion, 1956

Fig. 3 (above) Bee Ridge Presbyterian Church, Sarasota, Florida, main entry looking north, 1956

Fig. 4 (left) Venice/Nokomis Presbyterian Fellowship Hall, Venice, Florida, perspective drawing, 1956

continuing, endearing—imparting not only a sense of kinship with the present but a perception of the past and a vision of the future; and always pervaded with the relationship of God and man.[8]

During his eight-year tenure on the Gulf Coast, Lundy designed a multitude of building types, from single-family houses to office buildings and motels, but it is in the churches that he found a home for his deeply held reverence for structural logic and his judicious use of light, and where his search for a deeper origin of form and idea intertwined. His early experiments with intimate rooms for worship on the Gulf Coast of Florida provided the framework for later masterpieces such as the series of buildings for St. Paul's Lutheran congregation in Sarasota and the Unitarian churches in Westport and Hartford, Connecticut—all carefully maintained to this day.

The enduring legacy of Lundy's work through the sixties lies in his characteristic roof forms, which warmly embrace the spaces below and, of course, in his disciplined use of materials. Lundy seemed to understand the nature of a material for its essential and time-tested value, but he was also deeply engaged in experimentation and new developments in both wood and concrete construction through collaboration with industry, material fabricators, and the leading engineers of his generation. He kept abreast of the latest material testing research and innovations in structural design to extend the perceived limits of new and traditional material assemblies. For Lundy, each project had an optimal solution and a related material logic. For instance, of concrete he wrote, "I think to use concrete as an expedient rather than for its truth, is wrong. If it is right for the place and for the use, good."[9] This ethic was firmly planted during his graduate education and became further developed in practice. In his discussion of wood, he was able to express this concern in the context of American architecture:

In an age of complete uncertainty and tension, it is reassuring and universally appealing to all Americans to be reminded of their great heritage—the beautiful old wood structures of New England, still standing and beautifully preserved…[and the] traditions of beautiful wood buildings in the US like Howard Green's work in California—[with] some of its Japanese derivations. When you talk about fundamentals and timeless beauty, you reach everyone, I think. Wood is basic and is our heritage.[10]

To Lundy, it was clear that every material has an internal logic, which needs to be carefully ascertained and then applied logically.

After his early experiment with glue-laminated wood beams and wood decking in the Sarasota Chamber of Commerce building, Lundy situated the sheltering wood roof form in an array of variants, in spaces of worship in and around Sarasota, including St. Andrews in Dunedin, and the Church of the Holy Comforter in Treasure Island. During the late 1950s St. Paul's Lutheran Church contracted with Lundy to design a building complex, which included Fellowship Hall (fig. 7), an education building, and a sanctuary. Lundy's productive working relationship with the parishioners extended for more than ten years, until the completion of the main sanctuary in 1969.

Upon acceptance of the master plan by the St. Paul's congregation, construction began on Fellowship Hall, which would also serve as the worship space until the introduction of a larger sanctuary building (fig. 5). In Lundy's Fellowship Hall, the wood structural elements rise effortlessly from the stone-clad piers. The interior space is reminiscent of the inverted hull of a wooden ship, graciously sheltering the fellowship. Uninterrupted glazing connects the interior to the north and south porticoes. Ample illumination at the east entry logically contrasts the minimal introduction of light into the west chancel (fig. 7). As necessary, narrow steel columns assist the lofted ascending beams at the point of building enclosure. This interrelated wood, steel, and concrete masonry structural system creates the unique impression of the roof rising and suspending simultaneously, or perfectly balancing tension and compression in a closed structural loop.

In this bilaterally symmetrical plan and section layout, Lundy associates God with the vertical axis emphasized by upward-projecting, wood-laminated beams. Tongue-and-groove wood roof decking adds to the autumnal warmth of the interior and defines the horizontal axis at the low end of the roof in connection with the terrestrial life of the congregation, linking to the adjacent landscape. Pairs of splayed beams shelter porches to the north and south of Fellowship Hall, and rise high above the central gathering area (fig. 8). The interconnected assemblage of structure displays Lundy's affinity for the rational elegance achieved in Gothic cathedrals, with their pointed arches, ribbed vaults, and flying buttresses that freed the enclosure walls from primary load-bearing performance, allowing for large, translucent

8½"
ST. PAUL'S LUTHERAN CHURCH, SARASOTA, FLORIDA — VICTOR A. LUNDY, ARCHITECT
VIEW OF MAIN SANCTUARY — LOOKING EAST TOWARD CHANCEL END —
NOTE: All perspective drawings, etc, by the Architect

Fig. 5 St. Paul's Lutheran Fellowship Hall, Sarasota, Florida, early perspective looking toward chancel, 1959

Fig. 6 St. Paul's Fellowship Hall, Sarasota, Florida, looking south, 1959

Fig. 7 St. Paul's Fellowship Hall, Sarasota, Florida, view of side porch, looking east, 1959

Fig. 8 St. Paul's Fellowship Hall, Sarasota, Florida, looking west, 1959

expanses of stained glass. In the Fellowship Hall, Lundy directs structural forces through the combined effort of beams, columns, and piers, making possible ample glazing at the seating area and main entry, all protected from the sun by the generous roof (fig. 9).

As Lundy's work matured through the late 1950s, a unique strain of material development emerged in his roofing strategies in projects as diverse as St. Paul Lutheran Church in Melbourne, Gloria Dei Lutheran Church on Anna Maria Island, and St. Mark Lutheran Church in Orlando. In these projects, Lundy continued to test the spatial and structural limits of glue-laminated beam technology. St. Paul and Gloria Dei employ a radial organization that starts low with beams radiating horizontally from the center toward the outer edges and rises unbroken to a central tower culminating in a skylight. This arrangement allows the congregation to enter the sanctuary under a low sheltering canopy and follow the rising roofline into the church's main body. St. Mark Lutheran builds on this centralized plan and introduces a radial petal arrangement of shell structures surrounding a central chancel. The pulpit and chancel are nested below the wood petals and enclosed by a separate structural system of radiating glue-laminated beams rising to a pointed dome (fig. 10). The technical and spatial ambition of these soaring, interconnected structural wood shells, with glass infill between, stretched the limits of the local glazing industry's abilities, and eventually water found a way into the building, leading to its subsequent demolition. Even before then, Lundy had become uncomfortable with the increasing geometric complexity of the engineered wooden frame technique for creating enclosed watertight space, commenting that this strategy was becoming more appropriate for sculpture than architecture. One can see him testing the limits of his ideas in the iterative development of his work through the 1960s, with each perceived set of lessons and reflection allowing for clearer and more compelling work. The Lundy Studio continued to produce designs at a steady pace, and Lundy soon began to divide his time between offices in Sarasota and Manhattan.

With his return to the northeast, Lundy was in direct competition with the architects Philip Johnson, Pietro Belluschi, Carl Koch, and John Johansen for commissions such as the Unitarian Universalist Congregation in Westport, Connecticut. Given Lundy's impressive roster of built churches at the time it is hard to believe that he was not originally on the short list for this project. Lundy had ten completed and well-published churches, all in Florida, and one church in the northeast not yet in the design phase when the Westport Unitarian Congregation began its search for an architect. Lundy heard about the project at a Yale University conference and contacted the church directly, as the interviewing process was already underway.[11] The building committee agreed to a meeting with Lundy, and he was so captivating that the committee hired him to begin work on the project immediately.

Lundy met informally with many congregants to better understand the church's ethos and Unitarian program more deeply. The congregation believed that the Parsonage building should come first, to attract and retain a new minister. Lundy developed three versions of the residence for the detail-oriented congregation. Because the members of the congregation were so particular in their commentary during the design phase, Lundy began to think that this preliminary project would be his albatross. After exhaustive conversation and deliberation on the form and use of the stone and glass for the Parsonage, the congregation moved forward with no dissenting votes on the main sanctuary proposal, much to the surprise of the architect. From the development of Lundy's ideas in the "brains books," it was clear that the new worship space should provide appropriate acoustics for music and song, the possibility for active use of the complex all week long, including a location for the Westport Nursery School, and that the building should also function as a symbol of Unitarianism. Lundy's *Explanation of the Building* pamphlet, submitted as part of his proposal, outlines many of the initial aspirations:

> From the exterior, the effect will be mainly that of a simple fundamental shape with a timeless sense of beauty sheltering the hill, to be sheathed in copper, with the ridges running vertically to suggest uplift. The richness and the surprises occur mainly inside.
>
> Like the old Quaker meeting houses, this building is simple, built of honest durable materials and of good workmanship. Unitarians see their home as a "place" not a house, cathedral, ship, or church. The combining of all the

Fig. 9 St. Paul's Fellowship Hall, Sarasota, Florida, side view of wood ceiling, 1959

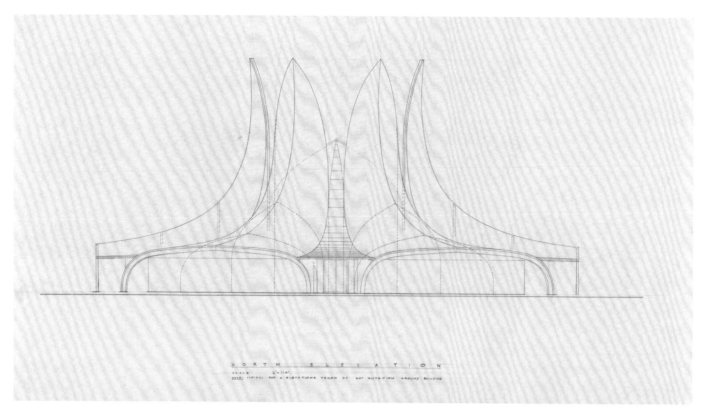

Fig. 10 St. Mark Lutheran Church, Orlando, Florida, elevation drawing, 1962
Fig. 11 First Unitarian Church, Westport, Connecticut, aerial view, 1961

Fig. 12 First Unitarian Church, Westport, Connecticut, church rendering, looking north, 1957

functions with their complications of purpose under one form that in part derives its shape from these requirements is in line with the traditional Unitarian meeting place.[12]

The experience of the building begins in the procession from the parking area to an entry court. Low, flanking eaves direct visitors into the social hall and sanctuary, with the roof rising boldly over the path toward the pulpit (fig. 2). From the parking lot to the sanctuary the site rises to a ridge of sixteen vertical feet and the roof soars sixty-five feet above the sanctuary. The building, with its two-hundred-foot-long sheltering wood roof, presents a powerful and efficient form that includes classrooms, social hall, sanctuary, and steeple all in one volume. In early renderings, a continuous stained-glass skylight of abstracted natural forms was included to separate the two roof sections in response to Lundy's conversation with parishioners and broader examination of Unitarian belief systems in relation to the natural world (figs. 13–14). Accordingly, the worship space is flanked by large panels of sliding glass, leaving direct visual and physical access to the grove of trees surrounding the building and allowing for a visceral relationship to the time of day and season of the year. For the architect and congregation, "the real sanctuary is the nature left there on the land"[13] (figs. 15–16). With phase one of the building finished in 1961, including the upper and lower area support spaces and the social hall, Rev. Arnold Westwood held the first worship service in the enclosed and air-conditioned portion of the new building. The sanctuary was protected by the dramatic prow of the wooden roof with no glass side walls, pews, or lighting. With the building's final phase of completion in 1965, the congregation held a dedication ceremony for the newly enclosed sanctuary, including a program of intimately choreographed music. With its rising wood ceiling, its lack of parallel walls to reduce reverberation, and a capacity audience, the space provided a warm acoustic tone that is still evident in worship and performances today (fig. 17).

In 1959 the East Harlem Protestant Parish acquired three open lots on East 101st Street and announced a call for architects to construct a new parish church in a tenement section of Manhattan that the New York Times Magazine described at the time as the worst in the city because of overcrowding, high crime rates, and a deteriorating building fabric.[14] Lundy was the only architect in attendance. The congregation had previously convened in several rented storefronts for services and also provided community assistance with addiction and tenant rights. Six-story derelict tenement buildings, slated for demolition, flanked the property. Despite this, the community was seemingly alive with joyfulness and was an essential part of this neighborhood—Lundy took the job.[15] The budget was low, just $200,000 for both the building and the costly foundation system required to resist settlement in the former marshland that underlies East Harlem (fig. 18).

The building committee agreed that the church must be compelling from all four sides and from above because of the multistory housing project that was slated to replace the surrounding tenements. Of great importance was to answer the vexing question of what a church should look like in the inner city.[16] Architect and congregation adamantly believed that the sanctuary should be at the apex of the composition, with nothing above it (fig. 24). Early studies included a skylight with colored glazing over the entire processional ramp and staggered Brickcrete masonry coursing for the sanctuary walls. To meet the community-centered needs of the pastor and congregation, a fellowship hall was located on the first floor adjacent to the main lobby with space dedicated to a Sunday school, neighborhood meetings, and outreach (figs. 19–23). In The City Observed: New York, Paul Goldberger outlined his experience of the building:

> Lundy avoids letting the form be too theatrical, which saves it, and one passes this church convinced that the sculptural form is a correct choice for this situation. It is a deliberate contrast to the oppressive red-brick public-housing towers nearby, and it speaks strongly of the notion that a religious house should stand for a certain irrationality of form—how else to know it from its banal neighbors?[17]

In the context of Manhattan, it might seem irrational not to continue the dense vertical urban fabric, but for a church that had been operating piecemeal in storefronts throughout the neighborhood of East Harlem, it was imperative to build a symbol of renewal. Lundy's striking sculptural solution is also a logical and ingenious response to program, budget, and site. The jury from the 1966 AIA Honor Awards agreed that:

> this remarkable building was outstanding among all the entries because it accomplished so much with so little.

Fig. 13 First Unitarian Church, Westport, Connecticut, worship space rendering, looking north, 1959
Fig. 14 First Unitarian Church, Westport, Connecticut, parish hall rendering, looking south, 1959

Fig. 15 (opposite) First Unitarian Church, Westport, Connecticut, worship space, looking south, 1961
Fig. 16 First Unitarian Church, Westport, Connecticut, worship space interior, looking north, 1961

Fig. 17 First Unitarian Church, Westport, Connecticut, high point of roof, looking west, 1961

Absolute economy of means was transformed into an asset. The entire character of the church, inside and out, seems completely consistent with its environment and purpose. Its austerity movingly expresses the strong structure of religious belief rather than the ornamental quality of ritual.[18]

Through architectural procession, powerful materiality, and a narrative of rebirth, Lundy was able to anchor this church to a community by designing a stable structural form that was hard on the outside but inviting on the interior, with its wood-clad ceiling reaching for the light. The architect created a sheltering arc-like space for a neighborhood in transition.[19] Goldberger wrote:

> The interior, like the exterior, has a restraint that brings dignity and prevents this from being as showy as one senses it might almost have been. A ramp leads up to the sanctuary, a tentlike space that climbs with a wood-ribbed roof to a corner skylight. You enter the space under a low ceiling, and only as you move into it do you see the soaring roof line, with a spot of natural light at the climax.[20]

Thankfully, Lundy was an architect who was willing to accept challenges that other professionals would not or could not accept, whether it was work for a congregation in an underserved neighborhood or maintaining an ethically clear trajectory for a lifetime of practice that linked a reverence for structure, light, and architectural discipline to serve both client and community.

In later religious buildings, Lundy advanced the suspended roof structure to a high level of specificity and sophistication. The nuanced articulation of the lightweight, hung-roof plane provided an antidote to the period's prevalent post-and-beam, flat-roof strategies and created the opportunity for unique interior spatial definition. As precedent-setting work, these developments necessitated the implementation of original material assembly systems employed within the building to address structural concerns related to the thin plane of the roof. The simultaneous focus on structural, spatial, and material conditions employed for this building typology, including that of the new worship space for the Unitarian Congregation in Hartford, Connecticut, provides fruitful primary source material for building science research (figs. 27–28).

In Hartford, Lundy organized the radial plan and structural solution for the meeting house around twelve concrete walls that rise out of the ground and into cantilevers supporting the sanctuary roof (fig. 25). A system of steel cables from John A. Roebling's Sons Company of New York spans between the radial walls to carry the four-by-six-foot, double tongue-and-groove, wood-decking roof system over the support spaces on the outer edge of the composition (fig. 26). A web of cables connected to the centralized cantilevered concrete walls lofts the tensile-supported roof over the worship space. A ring of illumination from clerestory openings surrounds the place of worship, while direct light entering the support spaces enters at ground level with views to the exterior (fig. 30).

Lundy carefully located the building on the inclined terrain. In his own words:

> The site lies on a gently sloping hillside overlooking Hartford, approached from on up the slope. It gives one the feeling of being able to see it from all directions and to see out from it in all directions. The concept is that many points of view draw together and become united in the center. One may start in one of many directions to reach the unity of the center; a unity of equality. The congregation specifically asked for a "closed" sanctuary; one that directs attention inward rather than outward. From outside, there is a sense of being able to enter from any direction; which is so. The building rises towards the center, the high points forming a ring of reverse skylights, which will throw colored light backwards upon the white walls of the sanctuary. A delicate ceiling tapestry of radiating thin wood members will further diffuse the light.[21]

The sanctuary is at the center of the composition in the form of a modified octagon. Its draping ceiling plane appears to gather light toward the center of the assembly area from the outside world into the space of Unitarian worship (fig. 29). This unconventional room with its slatted wood ceiling and lack of parallel walls provides a warm acoustical quality that supports the performance of a variety of musical traditions, which is essential to the Unitarian service (fig. 31). The only worship space with direct visual connection to the exterior landscape is a small, west-facing chapel named for Rev. Payson Miller, who oversaw the purchase of the new building site along with the planning and development of the new building. He was known to the congregation as a serious

Fig. 18 Church of the Resurrection, East Harlem, New York, exterior rendering, 1961
Fig. 19 (opposite, top) Church of the Resurrection, East Harlem, New York, roof geometry drawing, April 13, 1962
Fig. 20 (opposite, bottom) Church of the Resurrection, East Harlem, New York, building sections, October 15, 1962

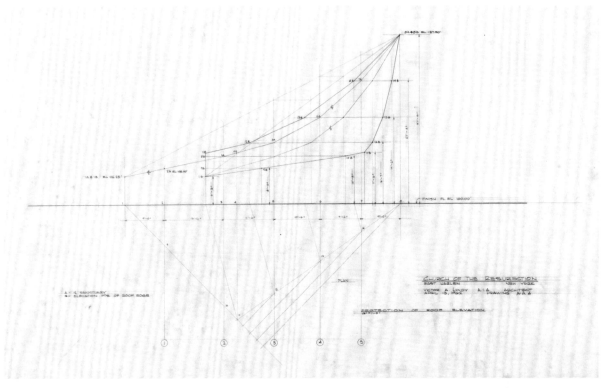

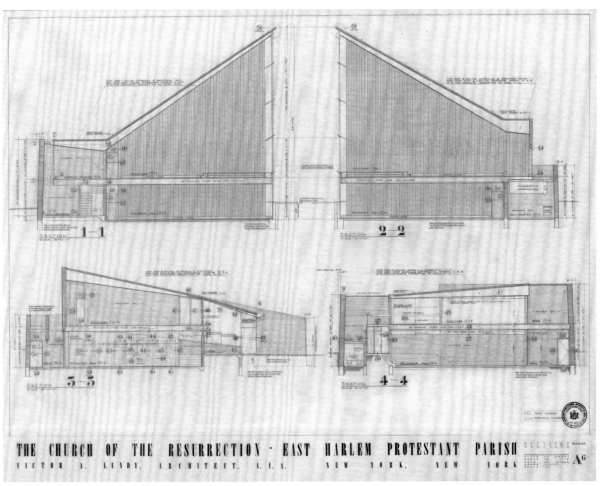

THE CHURCH OF THE RESURRECTION · EAST HARLEM PROTESTANT PARISH
VICTOR A. LUNDY, ARCHITECT, A.I.A. NEW YORK, NEW YORK

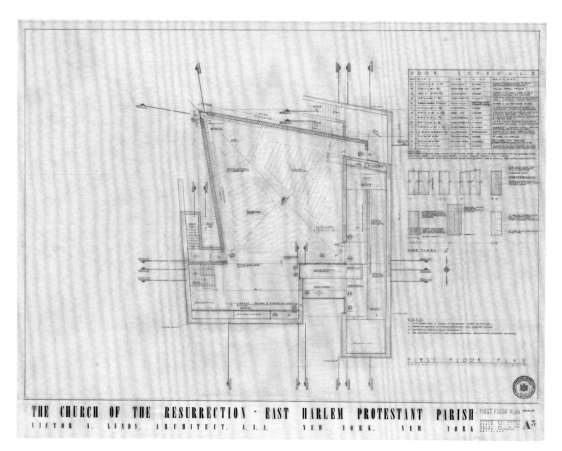

THE CHURCH OF THE RESURRECTION · EAST HARLEM PROTESTANT PARISH
VICTOR A. LUNDY, ARCHITECT, A.I.A.   NEW YORK, NEW YORK

FIRST FLOOR PLAN

A3

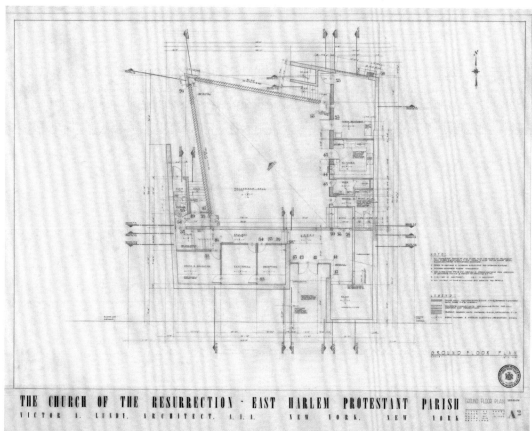

THE CHURCH OF THE RESURRECTION · EAST HARLEM PROTESTANT PARISH
VICTOR A. LUNDY, ARCHITECT, A.I.A.   NEW YORK, NEW YORK

GROUND FLOOR PLAN

A2

Fig. 21 (opposite, top) Church of the Resurrection, East Harlem, New York, first floor plan, October 15, 1962

Fig. 22 (opposite, bottom) Church of the Resurrection, East Harlem, New York, ground floor plan, October 15, 1962

Fig. 23 Church of the Resurrection, East Harlem, New York, ramp to sanctuary, 1965

man with an optimistic outlook. In a sermon, "Mysticism for Thoughtful People," he connected his all-encompassing conception of religion to the new sanctuary: "When we feel that something has become a whole, that it has become a holy thing, that it has found the place in life which it is intended to have, we have an experience of mysticism."[22]

The building solution for Hartford, in some ways, continued the development of Lundy's centralized plans for places of worship in Florida, but Hartford provided a distinctive outcome. In this case, the architect was adamant in his aspiration to link built form with the theological tenets of this particular congregation. The building committee requested a closed or internal sanctuary with a strong inward focus, and Reverend Miller articulated an interest in a building that symbolized the belief that all religions are but so many paths to a single, all-pervading reality. From the exterior, the twelve radiating concrete piers begin low in the landscape and rise toward the center of the composition, creating a thoughtful frame to the sky. It is not difficult to imagine the building geometry focusing various lines of inquiry inward toward the assembly. The ceiling of illuminated tracery metaphorically lowers the sky over the gathering, creating an intimate and inspiring place for both reflection and action.

For the larger tensile roof of the St. Paul's Lutheran sanctuary building in Sarasota, Lundy continued consultation with a structural engineer, Fred N. Severud, to achieve an elemental and highly principled space of worship[23] (fig. 34). Lundy wrote,

> I wanted a form that developed logically out of engineering, proportions, dimensions, and purpose. The result is a tent form, one of the most ancient of enclosures. And the promise of the form outside is fulfilled inside. The building is essentially one clear-spanned space, 90 ft. wide by 139 ft. long by 50 high at the center.…I tried to make the space an uninterrupted volume sheltered by a great curtain of wood—without an insistent pattern of structural framing to break it up.[24]

The sanctuary's defining feature is a hung wooden roof. To achieve this curvature suspension structure, the architect and the engineer designed an ingenious edge condition at the apex. To support the roof on suspended cables, the Severud-Perrone-Sturm-Bandel consultancy proposed a hybrid truss composed of a continuous, and relatively slender, steel ridge beam with eight triangular frames spaced eighteen feet apart. Within the open frames, two steel cables in tension are attached to the base of the triangular frame to brace against horizontal wind loads. Also, steel cables in tension are connected to the sides of the open frames along a parabolic curve to reinforce the ridge beam at midspan. To further resist wind uplift forces, taut steel cables span the worship space and connect the two halves of the roof.[25]

Cast-in-place concrete walls to the north and south provide privacy for the interior and support the steel ridge beam above. The end walls are angled for stability and trace the catenary curve of the steel-cable roof structure in profile as the wall interfaces with the roof system. Plastic-coated plywood panels measuring four feet by twelve feet define the concrete formwork pattern of construction ornament along with a systematic form-tie pattern. Concrete is shaped by wood, and its impression on the surface defines the modular logic imprinted on the walls. Through careful detailing, wood technology and its application imbue this building with a distinctly human scale and a connection back to the process of construction.

Upon entry from the south, congregants are welcomed into a vestibule that allows access both up to the balcony and around a service core into side aisles to the east and west of the worship space at the low point in the roof profile (fig. 32). The adjacent structural piers align with the sidewalls and a slice of light separates structure from enclosure. The first view of the worship space is on a diagonal axis with the roof soaring up toward the ridge truss. Light enters from above the chancel through a thin slot of glazing between the northern roof edge and concrete end wall (figs. 34–36). Lundy is keen to allow natural illumination strategically into the worship space, linking structure and light to the sacred and serene. He writes:

> I am very concerned these days with the control of light. In the St. Paul's Sanctuary, I wanted to make a great, cool, dark space—a place of shade in contrast to the persistent brightness outside….So there is a burst of light at the beginning, where one enters, and light at the end of the

(continued on page 127)

Fig. 24 (previous) Church of the Resurrection, East Harlem, New York, view of sanctuary at roof apex, 1965
Fig. 25 (above) First Unitarian Congregational Society, Hartford, Connecticut, 1964
Fig. 26 (right) First Unitarian Congregational Society, Hartford, Connecticut, exterior view of side porch, 1964

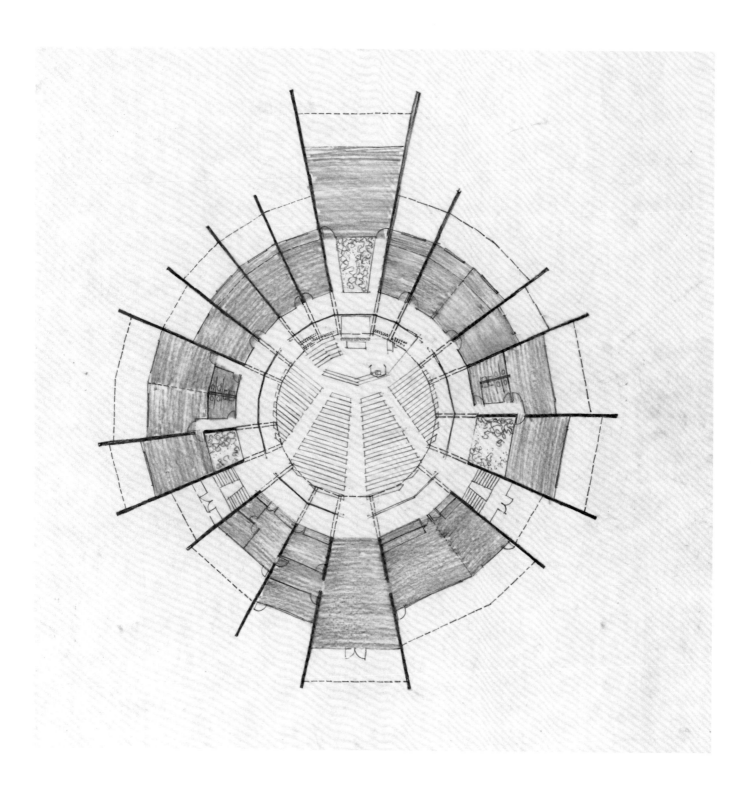

Fig. 27 First Unitarian Congregational Society, Hartford, Connecticut, floor plan, 1962.
Graphite on paper, 37 x 34 inches

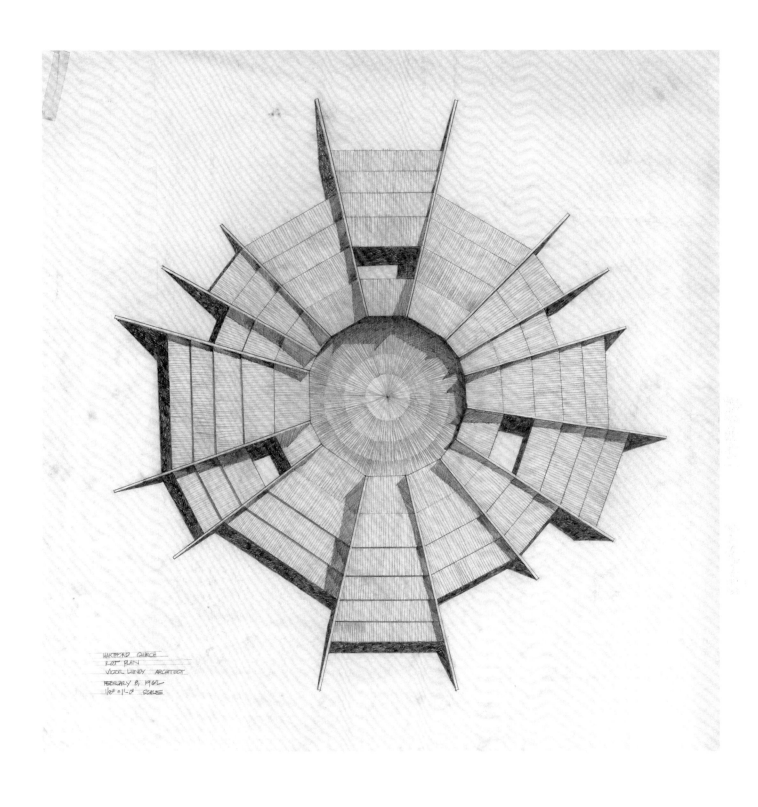

HARTFORD CHURCH
ROOF PLAN
VICTOR LUNDY ARCHITECT
FEBRUARY 8, 1962
1/8" = 1'-0" SCALE

Fig. 28 First Unitarian Congregational Society, Hartford, Connecticut, roof plan, 1962.
Graphite on paper, 34 x 36 inches

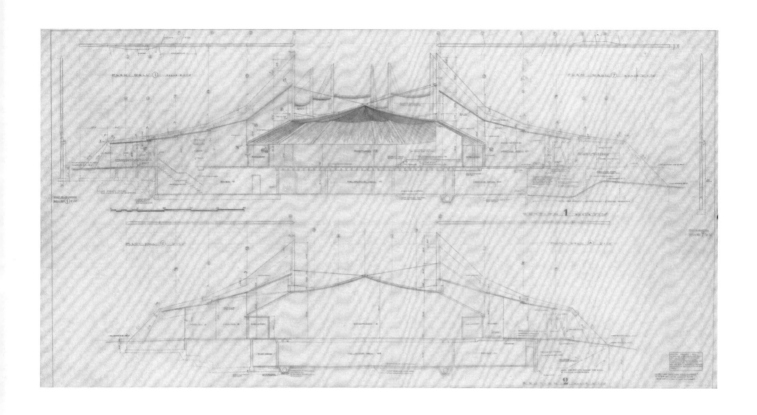

Fig. 29 (previous spread) First Unitarian Congregational Society, Hartford, Connecticut,
worship space looking north toward chancel, 1964

Fig. 30 (above) First Unitarian Congregational Society, Hartford, Connecticut, building section drawings,
December 7, 1962

Fig. 31 (opposite) First Unitarian Congregational Society, Hartford, Connecticut, interior view
toward pulpit and organ, 1964

Fig. 32 (opposite) St. Paul's Lutheran Church Sanctuary, Sarasota, Florida, interior entry hall, 1970

Fig. 33 (above) St. Paul's Lutheran Church Sanctuary, Sarasota, Florida, main entry, looking northeast, 1970

Fig. 34 (following spread, left) St. Paul's Lutheran Church Sanctuary, Sarasota, Florida, looking north, 1970

Fig. 35 (following spread, right) St. Paul's Lutheran Church Sanctuary, Sarasota, Florida, view of wood roof/ceiling, truss, wall, and skylight intersection, 1970

sanctuary, where the word is spoken from the pulpit and where the monolithic granite altar, polished on top and flame treated at the sides, stands.[26]

During the design process, Lundy and Severud dedicated themselves to the creation of a clear and irreducible spatial idea anchored by a structural and material condition that is inseparable from the place of worship (fig. 35). Technological and engineering solutions facilitated the architectural ideal and expanded the impact of the overall spatial experience. Through the metaphor and physical presence of the archaic tent-form, the architect was able to provide a meaningful space for contemplation and define an architectural language that continues his exploration of the sacred with a room for worship that feels simultaneously ancient and modern in its origin.

With over fifty years separating us from these first constructions, we have the critical distance necessary to understand this remarkable body of work in context. The sixteen churches designed by Lundy are technologically precise with sophistical material strategies, but the resultant spaces are more than the sum of their constituent parts. Victor Lundy was at the forefront of a generation that deeply explored the history of architecture and integrated that lineage into the work. In Lundy's case, the knowledge became embedded in his mind and hand through a lifetime of systematic travel around the world. We are fortunate that the artifacts of his work are available to us at the Library of Congress, through sketchbooks, drawings, construction documents, writings, and photography. Of course, Lundy's original vision is most directly visible in his buildings, the churches in particular, which form a rare synthesis of architecture, engineering, natural lighting, and landscape that serve and inspire many congregations to this day.

Fig. 36 St. Paul's Lutheran Church Sanctuary, Sarasota, Florida, side view of wood ceiling showing steel cables, 1970

United States Tax Court Building

Joan M. Brierton and Sarah A. Garner

The Tax Court Building deals in the generalized and time-less sense of balance, order and serenity that is genuine classicism. It meets the challenge of today's expression and technology as a prime creative objective. It is heart, hand and mind working together for man's most durable testament.

—Ada Louise Huxtable, "Architecture: Full Speed Forward"

In June 1965 Karel Yasko of the US General Services Administration (GSA) placed a call to the New York City office of Victor Lundy. His request soon proved pivotal to Lundy's career. The government was planning a new building to house the US Tax Court in Washington, DC, and Yasko wanted Lundy to take the lead. A few days later Lundy traveled to Washington to meet with GSA and associate architects William Lyles and Louis Wolff of Lyles, Bissett, Carlisle and Wolff. In August 1965 the contract was signed, and Lundy began preparing the design concept[1] (fig. 2).

Although Lundy later recalled his first conversation with Yasko as coming "out of the blue," it was the result of a deliberate, new approach to federal architecture that had begun several years earlier. Established in 1949 to improve economy and efficiency by streamlining administrative services within the federal government, GSA subsumed the roles of multiple agencies, including the Public Buildings Administration within the Federal Works Agency. A new division called the Public Buildings Service (PBS) became responsible for design, construction, repair, alterations, and management of most civilian federal buildings nationwide. Throughout the 1950s, PBS concentrated on completing projects that had been put on hold during World War II, including the expansion of the State Department headquarters in Washington, DC, and the redevelopment of the city's southwest neighborhood as a federal enclave. PBS struggled to alleviate an overwhelming problem, namely, that war and the Great Depression had instigated a fourfold increase in the number of federal workers, and the government needed more office space.[2]

Yasko joined GSA in late 1962 as special assistant to the commissioner of public buildings. He took on a role that had developed during the mid-nineteenth century in the US Department of the Treasury, which was responsible for public building design and construction for nearly a century before its responsibilities were transferred to the Federal Works Agency, and subsequently to GSA. The Office of the Supervising Architect of the Treasury Department oversaw many of the most important American buildings of the nineteenth and twentieth centuries, from Alfred B. Mullett's

Fig. 1 US Tax Court Building, interior of Great Hall, from below, 1975

Fig. 2 Sketch of elevation, ca. 1965

State, War, and Navy Department Building in Washington, DC, to Cass Gilbert's US Custom House in New York City. At the time the office was established in 1852, the government had constructed only a handful of classically inspired buildings, and the country had few professional architects.[3] A centralized government architectural office made sense. Over time, however, the numbers of both federal buildings and architects rose into the thousands. Two themes emerged that dominated the debate surrounding public buildings for decades: the issue of quality—and often the lack thereof—and of who should design them.

During the mid-nineteenth century, most federal building designs were developed in Washington, DC, far from their intended sites, with an eye toward standardization and streamlining. Government architects favored styles with historical antecedents. Influenced by the work and writings of the Italian Renaissance architect Andrea Palladio, Robert Mills designed the 1842 General Post Office in Washington, DC, with a monumental marble facade, centered temple portico, and colossal Corinthian columns with capitals referencing the Roman temple of Jupiter Stator. In designing the US Pension Building during the 1880s, Montgomery C. Meigs looked to Antonio da Sangallo's Palazzo Farnese in Rome, using alternating triangular and segmental pediments over the windows on the low brick facade. This early classicism briefly gave way to Victorian designs before regaining its popularity, first with Beaux-Arts

classicism between the 1890s and 1910s, and then with modern or stripped classicism, which became uniquely identified with public architecture during the early twentieth century. Staff in the supervising architect's office prepared plans for similar, and occasionally identical, buildings around the country, whose monotony and lack of innovation drew criticism from the increasingly influential architectural profession. The first legislation that allowed the federal government to use private architects for public building design was passed in 1893, marking the beginning of an era in which design responsibilities cycled between government and private architects.[4]

By the 1950s, after years of conflict, private architects had finally superseded government architects, and GSA evolved into the role of manager as opposed to designer. The Public Buildings Act of 1959 was passed to alleviate the severe shortage of office space, and GSA began a construction campaign that, between 1960 and 1976, produced seven hundred projects across the United States.[5] The buildings constructed through this immense effort soon received criticism for their lack of innovation, evoking some of the concerns directed toward preceding generations of federal architecture. This time, however, the recurring quality issues had escalated beyond just architectural conservatism. GSA's contextual study of the era, *Growth, Efficiency, and Modernism: GSA Buildings of the 1950s, 60s, and 70s*, notes that as private architects took over design

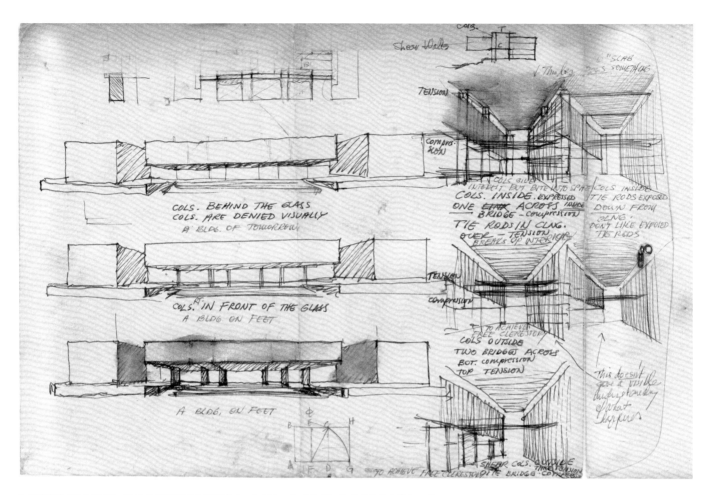

Fig. 3 Sketch on envelope, 1966

Fig. 4 Sketch of massing, from Lundy's brains book, ca. 1965

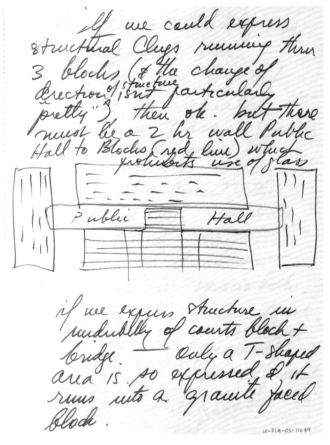

If we could express structural clues running thru 3 blocks (& the change of direction (of structure) isn't particularly "pretty") then ok. but there must be a 2 hr wall Public Hall to Blocks (red line) which prohibits use of glass

if we express structure in underbelly of courts block & bridge. — Only a T-shaped area is so expressed & it runs into a granite faced block.

Public   Hall

LC-DIG-dS-11089

Fig. 5 Plan sketch with notes, from Lundy's brains book, ca. 1965

responsibilities, the "lines of demarcation were soon blurred" between federal office buildings and private office buildings.[6] The symbolic government presence of earlier public buildings, easily recognizable through the use of high-quality materials and prominent, ceremonial entrances and spaces, had all but disappeared. Federal buildings morphed into glass towers and monolithic office blocks.

President John F. Kennedy was inaugurated in 1961. Disappointed by the state of federal architecture, he appointed the Ad Hoc Committee on Federal Office Space to advise his administration on space needs. In June 1962 the committee issued its findings in a report that included the "Guiding Principles for Federal Architecture," written by Daniel Patrick Moynihan, who was then assistant secretary of labor. The "Guiding Principles" set forth a three-point policy for federal architecture, stating that (1) buildings will "reflect the dignity, enterprise, vigor, and stability of the American national government"; (2) the government "should be willing to pay some additional cost to avoid excessive

uniformity in design of Federal buildings"; and (3) "the choice and development of the building site should be considered the first step of the design process."[7] Yasko began implementing the "Guiding Principles" a few months later, and these directives undoubtedly reinforced his decision to hire leading and forward-thinking architects for prominent commissions—including the retention of Walter Gropius for Boston's John F. Kennedy Federal Building, Ludwig Mies van der Rohe for the Chicago Federal Center, Marcel Breuer for the US Department of Housing and Urban Development headquarters in Washington, DC, and Victor Lundy for the US Tax Court Building (fig. 3).

The US Tax Court, originally the US Board of Tax Appeals, was created by the Revenue Act of 1924. The court consists of nineteen presidentially appointed judges, with a mission to provide a national forum to resolve disputes between taxpayers and the Internal Revenue Service (IRS). After it was completed in 1935, the IRS Building in the Federal Triangle housed the Tax Court. By the 1950s overcrowding and a desire to separate judicial powers from the IRS led to discussions about the construction of a building for the Tax Court. In 1962 Secretary of the Treasury C. Douglas Dillon wrote to GSA administrator Bernard L. Boutin to emphasize the inadequacy of accommodations in the IRS building and the growing concern over the appearance that the Tax Court was an arm of the IRS, when in actuality it was the respondent in litigation brought before the court. In response, GSA prepared a prospectus under the Public Buildings Act of 1959, and Congress approved it in 1963. The Tax Court would receive its first dedicated courthouse[8] (fig. 4).

True to the "Guiding Principle" that the site should be the first consideration in the design process, a location at Second Street and Indiana Avenue in Northwest Washington had already been selected by the time Lundy was brought into the Tax Court project in 1965. (Before choosing this site, GSA had considered and rejected a number of others, including Lafayette Square near the White House, the area between Ninth and Tenth Streets where the planned Federal Bureau of Investigation building was to be sited, and a parcel near the Potomac River, south of the present-day Kennedy Center.) During his June 8, 1965, meeting at the GSA building, Lundy wrote that the Tax Court would be located "in the shadow of the Capitol," and then carefully noted the complex design review process the project would undergo because of its Washington, DC, location:

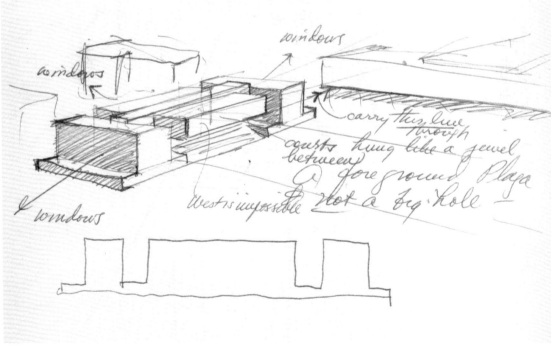

Fig. 6 Conceptual sketch of Great Hall, ca. 1965
Fig. 7 Sketch with notes from Lundy's brains book, January 6, 1966

1. The Fine Arts Commission must rule on it
2. The National Capital Planning Commission
3. Pennsylvania Avenue Commission
4. For the courts—must meet their approval—GSA handles

Several of architecture's leading thinkers were members of the Commission of Fine Arts at that time, and Lundy jotted down their names as well: Gordon Bunshaft, John Carl Warnecke, William Walton, and Aline Saarinen.[9] Despite Lundy's note that GSA would "handle" the planned tenant, he ultimately worked closely with the members of the Tax Court's building committee, responding to their requirements and vision, and also appealing to them directly for support in materials selection and other decisions.[10] In the process, personal relationships and deep mutual respect developed between Lundy and the committee, strengthening the investment and commitment each held in the project.

The Tax Court Building was to be a departure from Lundy's previous work, and was his first and only courthouse. The project had complex requirements and demanding space needs, including "3 court rooms with all attendant facilities, Robing Rooms, Press Rooms, Conference Rooms, Toilets, Counsel Rooms, Witness Rooms, Stenographic, Reporting, Communications, Health Unit, Loading Dock, Cafeteria, and Garage for 95 cars." The design team was told to fit all these spaces into a small site between the Federal Home Loan Bank Board Building and the proposed Department of Labor Building, all while staying within the city's then 110-foot height limit.[11] On November 16, 1965, Lundy, Lyles, and GSA presented the proposed design for the Tax Court Building to the Commission of Fine Arts. The members disapproved, concluding that the building warranted more space and recommending to GSA that changes be made "both on selection of site and on the basic approach to an architectural solution for the program."[12] Both Lundy and Judge William Fay, chairman of the building committee for the Tax Court, concurred that the site was problematic and not befitting the courthouse.

Within a month, the Tax Court and GSA had selected an alternative site on the east side of Second Street between D and E Streets in Northwest Washington, and instructed the architects to prepare a new design scheme. On December 15, 1965, Charles H. Atherton, secretary of the Commission of Fine Arts, presented the new design to the commission members. The building would include "a hall of justice in the center section of the building which would connect all the various components. Planned as an open well, the hall would have a corridor along each side and a clerestory would permit light to filter down through this area"[13] (fig. 1). Lundy's ability to capture and use light to define and enhance the experience of space would be realized now on a monumental level. The commission commended Lundy for the improved design and approved the preliminary plans. In 1966 Congress appropriated $450,000 for the initial engineering and planning.[14]

On November 15, 1966, Lundy presented the final design scheme for the US Tax Court Building. The models and plans indicated a six-story building—an inspired arrangement of solids and voids—with a massive courtroom block cantilevered over a monumental stair (figs. 7–8). A formal plaza to the west running perpendicular to the expansive horizontal building site was integral to the design scheme. The Commission of Fine Arts approved it the following day, and Chairman Walton congratulated the architect on "achieving the Commission's aim, an excellently designed building."[15] The project was ready to begin.

But while the Tax Court Building was undergoing design reviews, the United States was at war. Federal funds were directed toward Vietnam, and the project was put on hold immediately after the design was approved. During the next few years, however, leading publications began evaluating the unbuilt design—and their responses were overwhelmingly positive. Ada Louise Huxtable, architecture critic for the *New York Times*, who often castigated federal architecture, delivered exceptional praise for Lundy's work, describing it as "a progressive, sensitive, contemporary solution fully responsible to Washington's classical tradition and yet fully part of the mid-twentieth century."[16] *Architectural Forum* deemed it "one of the most daring structures, in terms of engineering, ever proposed for the capital."[17] In 1972 GSA selected the US Tax Court Building to receive an Honor Award in its first biennial Design Awards program.[18]

In 1971 the project was resumed, and GSA returned to the Commission of Fine Arts. Construction funding was now available, but the intended site was not. The Federal City College was temporarily occupying a portion of it, and the school could not be relocated until its permanent quarters were available. GSA decided that construction could not be delayed without risking the loss of funds allocated for the government's 1972 fiscal year. The solution, pursued to preserve both construction funding and the much-hailed

Fig. 8 Rendering, 1970

Fig. 9 Monumental staircase and cantilevered courtroom block, 1975

design, was to move the building one block westward, along Third Street, and rotate it 180 degrees.[19] This decision was not entirely without consequence: the rear of the building, rather than its intentional and monumental facade, would now face Judiciary Square, the historic courthouse district to the west of the original site. Lundy's vision of the original plaza as a "receiver to Judiciary Square" would never come to fruition.[20]

Groundbreaking ceremonies were held on July 31, 1972. On November 22, 1974, the fiftieth anniversary of the Revenue Act, a dedication was held in the public hall. During the ceremony, Judge William Drennen remarked, "I think that this beautiful and functionally graceful building epitomizes the role the Court has tried to live and portray for so long." Completed at a cost of $23,078,000, the building was occupied by employees on January 20, 1975.[21]

The bold US Tax Court Building conveys a sense of stateliness and daring unparalleled in modern federal architecture. Describing his design, Lundy stated, "What I've done is taken a monolithic block and broken it apart"[22] (fig. 9). Lundy conceptualized the site as a solid block of stone and divided its mass into four distinct building parts (or "blocks"), each definitive in form and function. The parts include a cantilevered courtroom block, weighing four thousand tons, flanked on each side by administrative blocks that house support functions for the court; to the rear, in the "chambers" block, are suites for each of the court's judges. The parts, devoid of fenestration and clad in flame-treated Royal Pearl granite from Georgia, are united by a central public space, the Hall of Justice, itself enclosed in bronze-tinted, heat-absorbing, glare-reducing glass with slim, bronze-anodized aluminum mullions. The palette used throughout the building includes board-formed, bush-hammered concrete; decorative teak grilles; tongue-and-groove hemlock panels; and plate glass. Lundy's skillful use and rhythmic repetition of these simple materials are

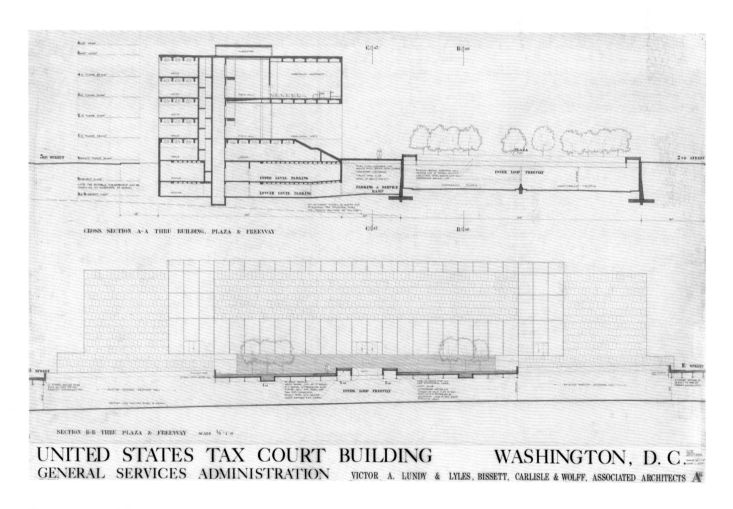

Fig. 10 Section and elevation, June 11, 1970

Fig. 11 (opposite) Great Hall, 1975
Fig. 12 Courtroom lobby, 1975

juxtaposed with the most sophisticated of structural systems, and together they constitute the architect's most singular and powerful modernist sculptural expression.

The cantilevered courtroom block, described in Lundy's project notes as "hung like a jewel" above the monumental entry, is made possible by an elaborate structural support system developed in partnership with New York–based Severud-Perrone-Sturm-Bandel, with whom Lundy frequently worked[23] (fig. 10). The two-hundred-foot-long, fifty-two-foot-wide courtroom block is cantilevered twenty-six feet above the building's entrance. With only six columns rising from the podium block to take the vertical load,

145 three-inch cables were used to anchor the courtroom block to the rear chambers block. Compression and post-tensioned pedestrian bridges with concealed cabling provide the necessary tensile force to anchor the block laterally.

These elegant bridges serve as critical elements in the building's circulation system, seamlessly connecting each of the four building blocks. The bridges use concrete-slab construction with tinted plate-glass balustrades capped with bronze strips—their functionality is not concealed but integrated into the building's aesthetic and elevated as a thing of beauty (fig. 1, page 128, and figs. 11–12).

Fig. 13 (previous spread) Courtroom with curved judges bench on the right, 1975
Fig. 14 Plaza under construction, ca. 1975
Fig. 15 (following spread) Facade, view from the east, photographed in 2006

Lundy's scrupulous attention to detail carried through to the courtrooms and to the building's more private spaces. In the courtroom block, there is a large, central courtroom, with smaller, near-identical courtrooms to the north and south (fig. 13). Bridging these spaces are teak-paneled vestibules exhibiting the same level of quality as the courtrooms themselves, each featuring a suspended stair with treads that appear to float as they ascend from one level to the next. There is not a standard feature to be found. Judges' suites, which included private chambers, a secretary's office, library, and individual office space for two attorneys, feature custom bookshelves, teak-veneered paneling, and exposed concrete ceilings. The entry to each suite is defined by a total-vision wall system of tempered, butt-glazed float glass. This partition serves as a striking transition between the private secretary's office beyond and the board-formed, bush-hammered concrete of the public corridor. Interior drywall partitions then separate the secretary's office from the library and the judge's chamber. These partitions extend to only eight feet in height. The remaining height, about two feet to the underside of exposed concrete tees, is butt-joint, clear-glass panels. The maximized natural light, borrowed through glass panels set above, was emblematic of Lundy's comprehensive and personalized approach to design. Even the artificial lighting exceeded all expectation in that it was customized, masterful in its approach to enhancing and simulating natural light, and fully integrated in its execution. Rows of exquisitely crafted, ceiling-hung pendants run in repetition throughout the suite. Housed in hemlock casing and suspended between concrete tees, the fixtures meet the glass partition panels with such precision they appear to float seamlessly from one space to the next. The result is a visual lengthening of space and further extension of borrowed light.

Despite the building's 180-degree rotation, the plaza was nevertheless constructed in its original location—now to the east of the building instead of the west—between 1975 and 1981. The plaza used the same granite as the building for its central raised reflecting pool and surrounding walkway (fig. 14). Lundy's Beaux-Arts training is clearly evident in his classically arranged design for the plaza and its grand, formal approach to the building.

Gleaming white classical buildings make up the architectural vocabulary of the National Mall and Pennsylvania Avenue in Washington, DC, their stately facades seldom straying from the federal government's most enduring architectural style. With the Tax Court Building, Lundy accomplished the seemingly impossible task of melding the principles of classicism with the innovation and boldness of the modern era. Writing for *Progressive Architecture* in 1976, Stanley Abercrombie rated the building as one of the best designs of the last fifty years, concluding:

> In this simple composition of smooth forms there is dignity; in this symmetry, there is repose; and in this almost unfathomable structural bravura there is clear evidence of engineering abilities not possessed by any earlier age of builders. Much has been written about the search for a building style both monumental and appropriate to our time, and some have doubted that such a style could exist or was even a valid goal. Now, and in Washington, of all places, it is built.[24]

The US Tax Court Building remains Lundy's most prominent public building and his only design in Washington. In 2008, when it was only thirty-four years old, the US Tax Court Building was listed in the National Register of Historic Places. To qualify for designation before it reached the fifty-year age threshold set by the National Register, the building had to have retained the highest degree of integrity and have met the standards for "exceptional" significance. The National Register concluded that the building was a nationally significant modern masterpiece, as it was one of a small handful of buildings derived directly from the Kennedy-era "Guiding Principles"; an exceptional design commissioned by the federal government; and the most structurally daring of the small group of buildings that adhered to the "Guiding Principles."[25]

In 2009, realizing an unprecedented opportunity to capture on film the recollections of the architect of this now-historic building, GSA began working with Lundy to create a documentary film on his life, work, and legacy. *Victor Lundy: Sculptor of Space* began with recognition of the Tax Court Building, but also presented his entire, previously undocumented body of work. Garnering nationwide attention, the film reintroduced Lundy to the architectural community and served as a catalyst for protecting and preserving the remaining works of this master architect. Reflectively referencing the US Tax Court Building in the film, Lundy states, "This building is a culminating work in my career as an architect. I'm very proud of the Tax Court Building. It's a building of its time and it's timeless"[26] (fig. 15).

United States Embassy, Sri Lanka

Donna Kacmar

Soon after establishing his New York City office in 1960, Lundy became aware of a new US State Department program designed to raise the quality of new federal buildings. In 1961 President John F. Kennedy asked Daniel Patrick Moynihan to head the Ad Hoc Committee on Federal Office Space to look at the issue of insufficient high-quality federal office space. The "Guiding Principles for Federal Architecture," set out in the committee's final report, stated, "Major emphasis should be placed on the choice of designs that embody the finest contemporary American architectural thought. Specific attention should be paid to the possibilities of incorporating into such designs qualities which reflect the regional architectural traditions of that part of the Nation in which buildings are located."[1] These "Guiding Principles" would later become the basis for the General Services Administration Design Excellence Program.

Lundy sent a letter expressing his interest and a brochure of his built work and qualifications to the State Department. He hoped to be selected to design a new embassy, and about a month later, he received a call asking if he would design an office building in Nigeria. Lundy was disappointed. He respectfully declined, saying that he would prefer to wait for an opportunity to design an embassy. Soon after, he was offered the opportunity to design the embassy in Ceylon (now Sri Lanka). This project would, like the US Tax Court Building, later be delayed by the Vietnam War.

Following a project briefing in Washington, DC, and a round of cholera, typhoid, and tetanus vaccines, Lundy traveled to Colombo, Ceylon, for the first time in January 1961.[2] The long series of plane flights to Colombo gave Lundy enough time to think about "the confidence that many men still unknown" to him had placed in him.[3] He wanted the embassy to be a reflection of the United States, and to be a "fine image in the highest sense," but he also wanted to understand the people of the place who would work there and how they would use the building.[4] He wrote in his journal about the future building occupants, "who would suffer through mistakes if they were made and would be lifted up in many ways in their daily lives if [the building were] successful."[5] Lundy was well aware that his client was the State Department, but he felt, most importantly, that "art and architecture are for people and the building must speak for itself and say something to them."[6]

Lundy extended this first trip to Colombo to include stops en route in Tehran, Isfahan, and Persepolis, in Iran; New Delhi, Agra, Jaipur, Fatehpur Sikri, Bombay (now Mumbai), Aurangabad, and the Ajanta Caves, in India; Mount Lavinia, Kandy, Polonnaruwa, Anuradhapura, and

Fig. 1 US Embassy in Sri Lanka, looking northwest, 1984

Sigiriya, in Ceylon; Angkor Wat, Cambodia; and Bangkok, Thailand. This was a serious introduction to a part of the world he had not yet experienced, and it gave him a better understanding of his assignment in Ceylon.[7] He was concerned that foreign "professionals" might influence how the country developed rather than allowing native Ceylonese creativity to evolve. He hoped Ceylon could have a leader like Jawaharlal Nehru, the first prime minister of India, to help it grab hold of its own future.

Upon landing in Colombo, Lundy immediately noticed the humidity and the "hotness so continuous there is no relief."[8] Lundy began to explore, trying to get a sense for the overall colors of the island, visiting its Ceylonese teak forests. His first impressions were of cerulean blue pools of water and brown teakwood, which inspired his visions of dark polished floors and buildings with large, gray stone bases. The painter in him also noticed how the orange, yellow, and off-white colors of the people's typical clothing stood out against the darkness of the wood and polished floors, and he sought to replicate this heightened contrast in materials and colors in his building.

Lundy knew of recent modern embassies that were "tinny," paper thin, and insubstantial, and he aspired to produce a "timeless fundamental beauty with substance."[9] He wrote in his journal:

> I have an awareness, I believe, of the obligations of my work, I'm very anxious to do honor to my country, to the people who have put their faith in me. I will try to design an embassy that isn't thin and skimpy, that can stand as a real, timeless symbol of what the United States stands for, and that I hope the Ceylonese people will love, I hope never to forget the big sense of what all this work is about.

He further wrote:

> Let a visit to the US Embassy be a refreshing, cool, memorable, happy experience—cool, efficient, beautiful, comfortable inside—lovely, strong, memorable outside—something to carry away with them.[10]

Many schemes were explored for the embassy. The site was relatively flat, in an urban area, between the busy Galle Road on the east and a railroad line on the west before the site opened onto the Indian Ocean. The first scheme, which Lundy developed in 1961, was a large rectangular block with

a sculptural exterior wall panel (figs. 2–3). Lundy sculpted foam to study the possible three-dimensional forms for the plan. Rex Hellmann, a straight talker from Foreign Buildings Operations (FBO), was Lundy's direct contact for the embassy project. Hellmann's role was to communicate the requirements for the embassy and advise Lundy on how best to proceed. Hellman recommended a simple, modern flat roof for the building.

For Lundy, the design of the embassy was not a smooth process. The project's scope was reduced several times, and it was often delayed when money and attention were diverted to other embassies in major cities such as Paris, London, and Helsinki. After Lundy's initial trip and first scheme, the project was put on hold because of the Vietnam War (as was his US Tax Court Building, which he had begun in 1965).

The FBO updated its embassy program on January 14, 1974, reducing the size of the building.[11] This was used as a starting point when the embassy project was rekindled in 1976. In the meantime, Ceylon had become a republic and changed its name to Sri Lanka. Lundy's work resumed again with a June 1976 trip back to Colombo.

At this point, Richard Gray from FBO began to question Lundy's ability to do the work, since, due to the lull in architectural work for his firm, he was now "in education" and since the original contract was initiated "ages ago." Gray said to Lundy that there was no question "that you're one of the great designers of this century" but also that the FBO was "not looking for great architecture, just something suitable," hinting at the importance of the limited construction budget.[12]

Lundy put together a first-rate team, including Colaco Engineers for the structural engineering and I.A. Naman + Associates, Inc. for the civil and mechanical engineering, yet FBO, still unsure that Lundy was capable of handling the project, wanted him to join forces with another firm to do the production work. Lundy fought hard to avoid this after his experience working with an architect of record for the US Tax Court Building in Washington, DC, where he ended up having to draw every detail himself. He knew it would be hard to get paid enough for his time for a project this size. Lundy explained that he had waited patiently for fifteen years and he was a better architect now than he was when he was initially hired. Eventually he convinced FBO that he could do the job. The contract was signed on May 12, 1977, and the design work began in earnest. The design of an

Fig. 2 Perspective sketch of first scheme, 1961
Fig. 3 Perspective sketch of first scheme showing porte cochere, 1961

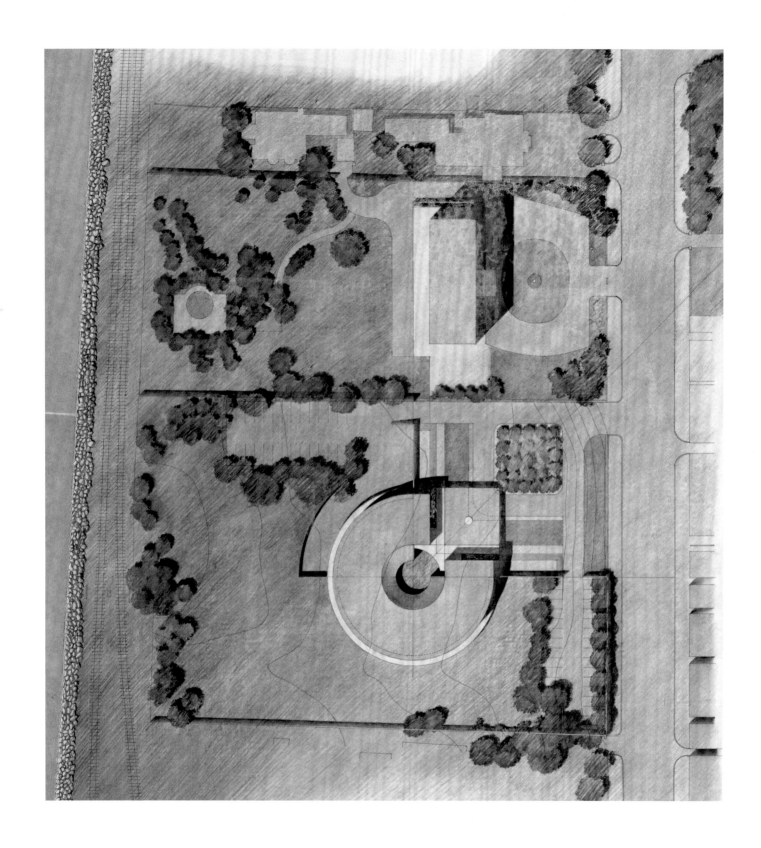

Fig. 4 Site plan of circular scheme, September 20, 1977

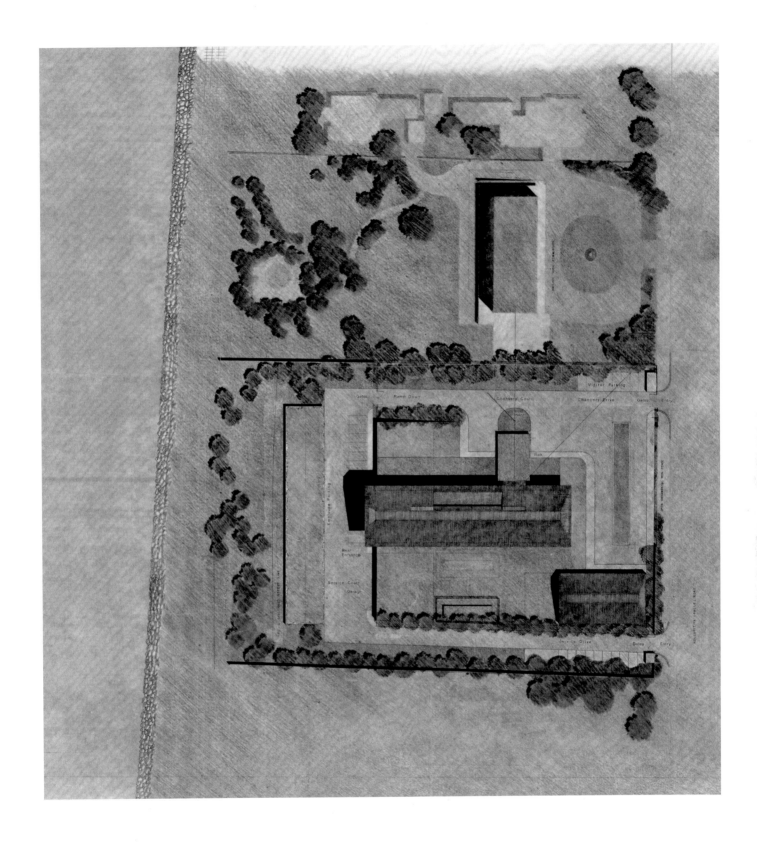

Fig. 5 Site plan of final scheme, November 29, 1978

embassy building required the input of many staff members and a review board that included Bill Caudill, O'Neil Ford, Joseph Esherick, and Bill Letheridge. In addition to overall design approval, many technical considerations, including separate vehicle and pedestrian entryways, varying types of clearance and security levels, egress routes, special air-conditioning requirements, and the inclusion of trash incinerators and generators that were atypical in a building this size had to be addressed.

A new scheme, with drawings completed on September 6, 1977, featured a building formed by three-quarters of a circle arranged around a courtyard that faced the Indian Ocean—an open-ended, visually inviting scheme (fig. 4). Ford, who was part of the review board, liked the scheme and its references to Vitadage, an ancient circular building at Anuradhapura. However, once Lundy learned of the specific requirements for US Marine guards and the security elements that would fill the plaza, the scheme was abandoned.

Lundy worked to develop yet another scheme that would both satisfy the State Department and be worthy of the people of Sri Lanka. On December 15, 1977, Lundy wrote, "Hurray!" in his notebook; the final scheme was approved.

Lundy made another trip to Colombo, August 7–20, 1978. A full day of meetings was set up with US ambassador W. Howard Wriggins and his staff to present the updated scheme.[13] Lundy wrote in his notebook:

> Prime Minister appeared to respond favorably to the basic idea of the building running East to West, allowing a green strip N[orth] and S[outh], the sense of preserving a feeling of connection between Galle Road and the sea[14] (fig. 5).

After the presentation, Ambassador Wriggins wanted time to meet with his staff. Later he told Lundy that he loved the design, but it reminded him of the country's ancient past. Wriggins felt that the building needed more than a flat roof to connect it to the contemporary cultural identity of Sri Lanka. Lundy agreed with this reaction and was elated to hear it. He told the ambassador that he knew exactly what to do and proceeded to make a sketch, right in front of him, of a building with sloped roofs. This was something Lundy had wanted all along, but it was Hellman of FBO who had encouraged him to make a simple flat roof (fig. 6). The final basswood model shows the sloped roof scheme (fig. 7). In 2014 Lundy donated this model to the National Building Museum in Washington, DC (fig. 8).

As the program and roof design were finalized, Lundy developed the technical aspects of the building, including its structural and mechanical systems, and researched the availability of specific concrete mixes and other building materials. As late as September 1, 1978, the FBO team was still discussing buying additional adjacent land for the site. By the October meeting in Washington, DC, the site was finalized, as was Lundy's architectural fee. Subsequent directives and notes from Hellmann asked for simple wood details that could be built locally.[15] The design development package was due in March 1979, and Lundy made another trip to Sri Lanka as the ground breaking was set to take place in September. However, the final drawings for the embassy were not issued until November 19, 1979 (figs. 9–11). Later, on January 11, 1980, Lundy was told of the need for a retrofit to the design to make it "fail safe" in case of political unrest. All embassies were being upgraded to reflect new safety standards, and the Sri Lankan embassy's roof would be required to support a helicopter in case of emergency evacuations and a few other modifications. The revised drawings, with the building modifications, were reissued on May 7, 1981.

Lundy considered the exterior materials carefully. He originally thought stone might be too austere and expensive. After investigating maintenance and other considerations, Lundy decided that sheathing the building in stone would give it the desired monumentality. This began a long process of visiting stone quarries in India, as there was no suitable granite in Sri Lanka. Eventually, in June 1980, he found the sand-colored stone he liked in an open stone quarry outside Hyderabad, South India, near the seaport of Tuticorin.[16] There, he saw firsthand how the stone was extracted from the quarry. When he identified a stone area he liked, workers outlined the block and marked the four corners by inserting metal corner markers. They then lit a fire on the stone surface and corners, heating and expanding the metal rods and cracking away the stone block until they could lift it out of the ground. Each piece of the rough-hewn stone cladding was cut by granite craftsman based on Lundy's drawings and shipped to Colombo.[17] The surface of each four-inch-thick stone piece was then bush hammered by hand.

Lundy loved incorporating local materials and techniques, and he used the handmade clay tile roofs he had seen on buildings throughout Sri Lanka in the embassy. The tile's curve was formed when the workers laid the clay on their thighs, and the roof tiles were installed by experienced

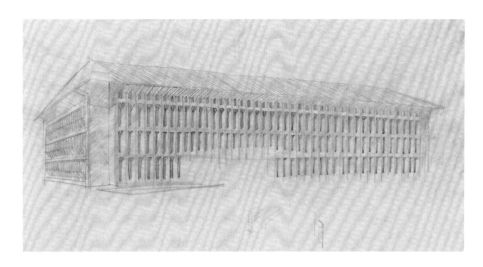

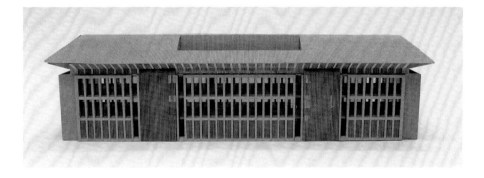

Fig. 6 (above) Sketch of final scheme, 1979
Fig. 7 (middle) Final model, from above, 1979
Fig. 8 (bottom) Final model, view of east side, 1979

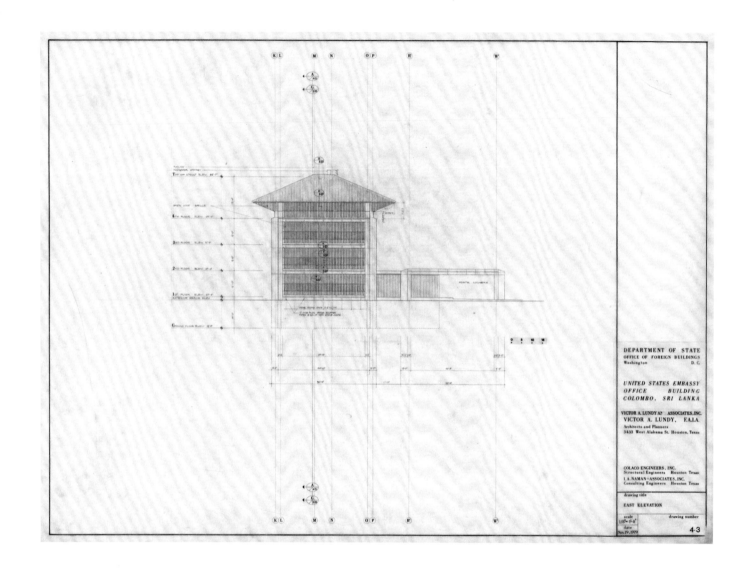

Fig. 9 Construction documents, front elevation, November 19, 1979

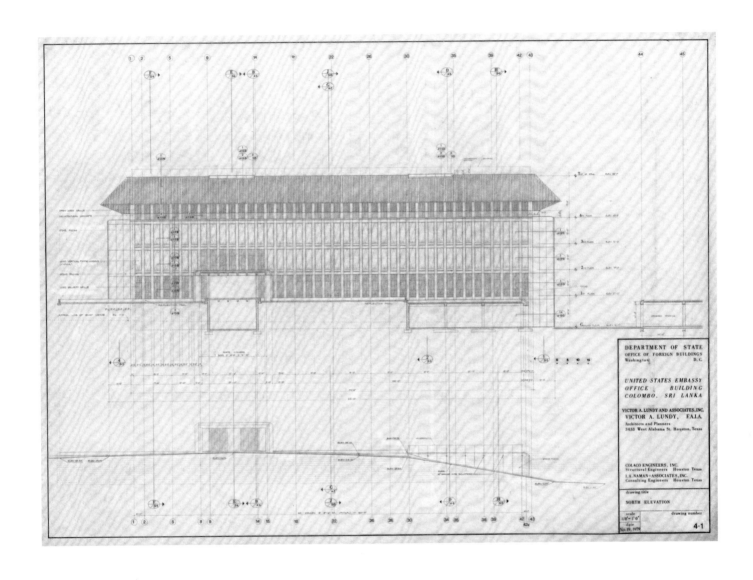

Fig. 10 Construction documents, elevation and section, November 19, 1979

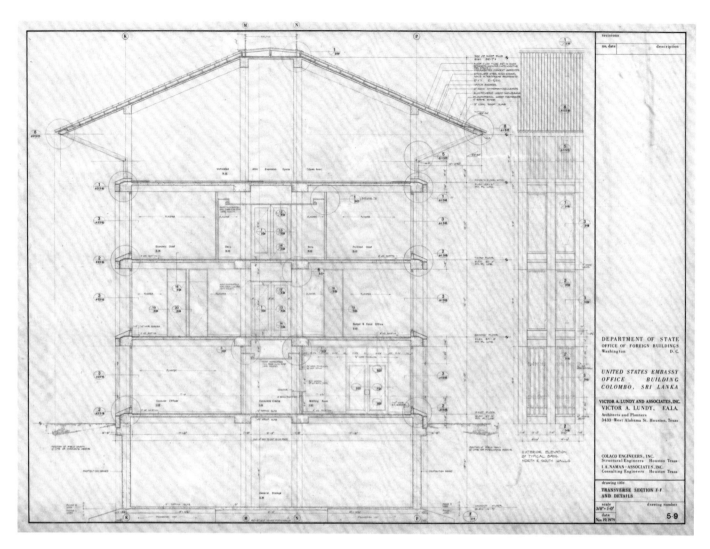

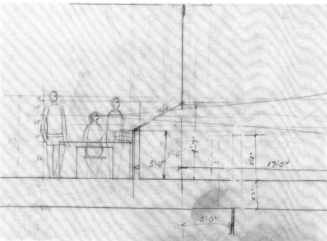

Fig. 11 Transverse Section F-F and detail, November 19, 1979
Fig. 12 Sketch of window screen, March 1, 1979

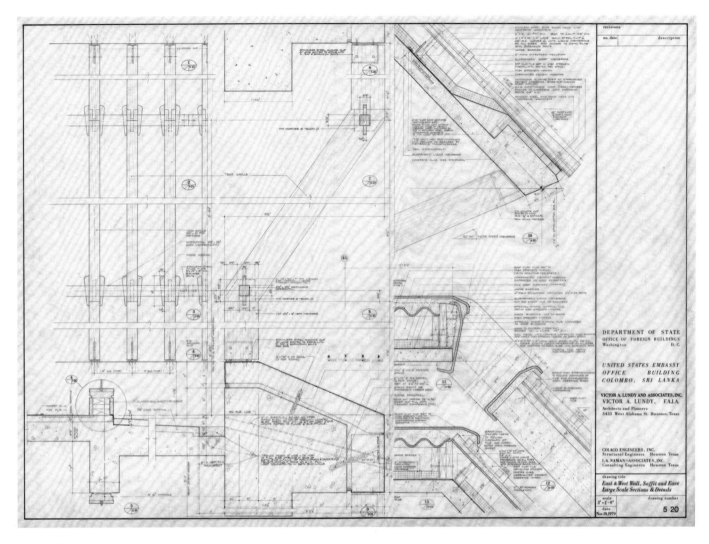

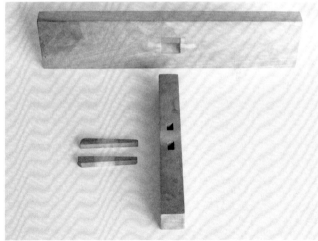

Fig. 13 (top) Soffit and eave large-scale sections and details, November 19, 1979
Fig. 14 (above left) Wood connection detail mock-up, photographed in 2017
Fig. 15 (above right) Wood connection detail mock-up, photographed in 2017

Fig. 16 Wood detail at balconies, 1984

Fig. 17 View of outer lobby, looking north to porte cochere, 1984

local craftsmen and set with a three-inch overlap in high-strength mortar. A membrane roof was placed underneath the tiles on top of the three-inch concrete roof slab. Additional engineering was required to transfer the relatively heavy roof loads to the concrete columns.

Teak was also used extensively in Sri Lanka, and Lundy appreciated how it weathered to a beautiful seaside gray finish—an effect he would try to employ in the embassy.[18] He had completed numerous sketches of the latticework of teakwood at the Padmanabhapuram Palace in Trivandrum, India, and on his first trip to India and Ceylon in 1961, Lundy had noted the traditional woodwork:

> I loved the perfect, intimate, small human scale, eaves that came down low, low, to kill bright glare and recognizing in some spaces that the sitter at tables needed a proper reference line for the sky. The sculptured teak fins carrying teak slats made a beautiful lacework of light in the narrow lookout porch bands on each tier of the main building. Their projecting cross section was for a reason: for lookout, protection, privacy, ease of observing without being observed, ventilation. The roofs in all cases were beautifully framed in wood—great, steep shelter and shade roofs that swept down to the low eaves.[19]

Early sketches show how Lundy studied the views enjoyed by both standing and sitting occupants at the windows and balconies he developed (fig. 12). His understanding of local details was transformed into the modern wood screens he designed for the windows in the embassy building. Lundy even made a prototype connection detail to show the Sri Lankans how to build the screens (figs. 14–15).

Embassy construction took one and a half years to complete, and the contract did not permit Lundy to supervise construction on-site. He did receive some photographs as construction proceeded and was allowed one last inspection trip when the building was finished. He wrote on May 13, 1984, in a note to his wife:

> When my taxi turned the corner and I knew I would finally see it, I *really* and truly did not know what to expect. It was either cardiac arrest or a shout of joy! It was a shout of joy! The stone is a handsome sand color, very light and delicate (close to what I wanted). The teakwood (Burma teak) details were all in place—though stained a strange orange color....The roof is superb. It looks *exactly* like my wood model, is sited beautifully, and all of Sri Lanka is talking about it.[20]

Fig. 18 Side view, looking south, 1984

Lundy was pleased with the exterior, except for one thing. He had wanted to let the teak of each window frame soften to the naturally weathered gray he so admired. Instead, all the teakwood was varnished. The shiny surface did not allow the subtlety he desired.

A similar finishing mistake was made on the interior. Lundy intended for all interior walls to be painted a beautiful flat white. Notes indicated a local grass-cloth to be installed on a few walls only in the ambassador's office, but workers interpreted this note to signify a color selection, rather than a material choice, and painted all the interior walls an off-white color. This muddied the intended crispness that Lundy desired.

The prominent face of the concrete frame building is oriented west, toward the sea. A side-facing porte cochere leads directly to an outer lobby and a double-height inner lobby. The large overhanging roof protects the building against rain and sun. The building's silhouette as it meets the sky was important to Lundy as he sculpted the roof.[21] The east and west roofs slope at a forty-five-degree angle to shed water quickly, a necessity in the tropical climate of Sri Lanka. The short end roofs slope at twenty-two degrees; the intersection of the roof ridges aligns with the building mass below. Open teakwood grilles on the underside of the roof connect visually to the grilles at the windows and balconies that provide security, privacy, and sun control. The extensive woodwork not only showcases the local craft but also brings a more human scale to the building, honoring the host country while demonstrating American strength.

The completed project was published in *Architecture* in July 1984, over twenty years after Lundy began work on the project. In 1988 the US Embassy in Colombo was selected from more than five hundred submissions and received the Federal Design Achievement Award, the National Endowment for the Art's highest honor in design. This building deeply honors the "Guiding Principles for Federal Architecture" established in 1962 for the General Services Administration Design Excellence Program and the subsequent architectural design criteria of the Department of State Foreign Buildings Operations. The building, some nine thousand miles from Washington, DC, and whose maintenance is directed by a continual rotation of staff, has not received the care it deserves. The building is now under threat of demolition as a new, larger embassy building is under construction on an adjacent site. The Bureau of Overseas Buildings Operations, a department within the US State Department, is in charge of the design and construction of new embassy buildings worldwide. According to its website, the bureau also maintains the "portfolio of legacy and culturally significant properties."[22] It remains to be seen if the bureau will live up to its self-stated responsibility.

Fig. 19 West-facing balcony, 1984

Houston Projects

Stephen Fox

After moving to Texas in 1976, Victor Lundy spent eight years teaching at what is now the Gerald D. Hines College of Architecture and Design at the University of Houston. In 1984 he accepted a position at the Dallas-based architecture firm of HKS. Until his retirement in 1998, Lundy lived in Houston and commuted to work in Dallas, becoming a design principal and vice president of HKS, in charge of such major corporate complexes as the GTE World Headquarters in the Dallas suburb of Irving (1991) and the sixteen-story, mixed-use Austin Centre in downtown Austin (1986).[1] Lundy also designed four buildings in Houston independently of his work for HKS: an art studio for his second wife, Anstis Burwell Lundy, in Bellaire, Texas (1984–85), a house for the two of them adjoining her studio (1987–88), a freestanding studio building for himself in a Houston warehouse district (1997–98), and a house in Houston's West End neighborhood for the interior designer Joan B. Miller (2002–3). Each building is a masterpiece. Lundy's skills at shaping space and building with precision and economy shine through as clearly in each of these buildings as in his earlier, more celebrated works.

The art studio for Anstis Lundy and the couple's adjoining house were built on a flat, half-acre lot in Bellaire, a separately incorporated, middle-income community adjacent to Houston. A simple shed in format, the art studio is a rectangle, with six eight-foot-wide structural bays along the long north and south sides and four six-foot bays along the shorter east and west ends. The studio's proportions—based on division into six-, eight-, and twelve-foot increments—suffuse the space with a sense of expansiveness.

A single volume inside, the studio is punctuated with a freestanding oval enclosure containing mechanical equipment and plumbing and lined with deep shelves on its exterior faces. The building's concrete floor slab is elevated two feet above grade on concrete piers. The studio's shape derives from its roof structure of seven elliptical, glue-laminated arches made of hemlock and supported by slender, steel-pipe columns embedded in the north wall and wood posts embedded in the south wall. The arches rise to frame a north-facing strip of clerestory windows. The interior walls and ceiling are white-painted drywall. In addition to the north-facing clerestory windows, the studio's western elevation opens to the deep backyard with sliding glass doors set below an internally exposed wood lintel. The exterior is faced with lapped Alaskan yellow cedar siding, now weathered; the roof vault is faced with a raised-seam metal sheathing.

The art studio is an architectural work of clarity, precision, and economy, which is apparent in Lundy's perspective

Fig. 1 Lundy House and Studio, Bellaire, Texas, back elevation, looking east, 1988, photographed in 2017

Fig. 2 Lundy House and Studio, Bellaire, Texas, front elevation of the house addition, 1988

ADDITION TO RESIDENCE
EAST ELEVATION   SCALE 1/2"-1'0"

VICTOR A. LUNDY ARCHITECT F.A.I.A.   701 MULBERRY LANE, BELLAIRE, TEXAS 77401

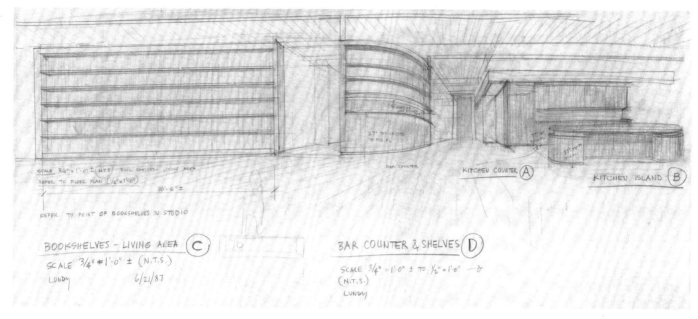

Fig. 3 Lundy House and Studio, Bellaire, Texas, interior sketch of the living and kitchen cabinetry, 1988

sketches and dimensioned drawings. The certainty with which he profiled the curvature of the roof and ceiling in both his perspective sketches and the measured drawing of the east elevation, and the articulate variation in line weight and intonation of the exterior study elevations, reveal the exactitude with which Lundy envisioned the studio.

When Anstis and Victor Lundy moved to Houston, they initially remodeled and occupied the existing house on the Mulberry Lane lot even though they intended to replace it with a new one. Lundy began to plan the new house as early as 1977, although the construction documents were not prepared until 1987. The house was completed in 1988, three years after the art studio. The Lundy House is astonishing in its simplicity and spatial sophistication. A one-story, flat-roofed pavilion, it is closed on the east-facing street side, where the projecting garage wing, with its lower roofline, is the most prominent element visible from the street (fig. 2). Although west is the most punishing orientation in hot, humid Houston, Lundy said that it also offered the best view into the wooded backyard (fig. 1). The house is extensively glazed on its rear, west elevation. Lundy's initial studies were for a rectilinear house, but Anstis Lundy observed that such a shape did not take advantage of the west view. So Lundy resorted to what he characterizes as an act of "instinctual design" unrelated to the governing structural logic of the

house. He inscribed a bold quarter-circle of floor-to-ceiling glass that in plan seems to scoop space out of the house but, experientially, sets interior space in motion with an extraordinary visceral charge. Everything about the design plays off this sweeping curve: the structural rationalism of the glue-laminated hemlock beams, which mark off eight-foot-wide bays with exposed steel-pipe columns; the Douglas fir ceiling deck; the floor of polished, two-foot-square limestone slabs; and the Luauan Philippine mahogany cabinetry in the open kitchen, which continues in a line of open shelves facing the passage to the studio (fig. 3).

The big curve was not the only innovation in the Lundy House. Lundy systematically dissolved planar continuity in the house's main space with floor-to-ceiling glass windows placed at strategic intervals. He introduced continuous clerestory glass in the kitchen, highlighting the intersection of the high-ceilinged roof of the house with the lower roofline of the garage and utility rooms. The rear fireplace wall, detached from the house's west end, seems to stand free in the backyard, framed by floor-to-ceiling glass panels and backlit by a concealed skylight. The Lundys' mixture of classic modern furniture, Oceanic and Asian art, and a few eighteenth-century pieces complement and stabilize the expansiveness of the living room. Lundy orchestrates spatial consistency with secondary moves that promote perceptions of rhythmic consistency: the way that the bookshelves

Fig. 4 (previous spread) Lundy House and Studio, Bellaire, Texas, living room, facing north, 1988, photographed in 2017
Fig. 5 (above) Lundy House and Studio, Bellaire, Texas, living room, facing west, 1988, photographed in 2017

Fig. 6 Lundy House and Studio, Bellaire, Texas, front facade, 1988, photographed in 2017

curve in plan to mirror the curved end of the kitchen island; the planar offsets in the entrance passage, where the protruding garage overlaps the ceiling fascia. This overlap causes the passage to narrow as one moves from the living room toward the front door and, conversely, to expand to welcome visitors.

Two bedrooms, each with its own bathroom, are sequestered in the house's northeast corner. Both face Mulberry Lane. Although they do not participate in the spatial drama of the living room, the bedrooms demonstrate the intricacy of Lundy's spatial imagination. Here, with less fanfare than in the great curved space, Lundy makes another imaginative decision, with the solid walls of the bedrooms rising eight feet and then continuing to the underside of the twelve-foot-high ceiling deck as transparent internal clerestories. Two enclosed bathrooms are introduced in these lofty spaces as subsidiary volumes, with banks of closets and built-in writing desks and shelves set adjacent to street-facing windows to spatially insulate the rest of the bedrooms and prevent them from feeling too exposed to the street. Lundy inserted one of the bathrooms inside the cylindrical corner opposite the kitchen. There the conjunction of functional particularity and volumetric experience displays economy, consistency, and concision. No condition is isolated merely to produce a formal gesture.

The orchestration of space in the Lundy House invigorates and excites: Just walking inside it is an exhilarating experience. The curved wall of glass surprises and opens one's perception of the interior volume. The space pulsates with the "generosity of spirit and radiance" with which Lundy and the children remembered Anstis Lundy after her death in 2009 (Fig. 1, page 162, and figs. 4–6).

Lundy's studio building is as astonishing as his house, its simplicity and straightforwardness notwithstanding. A freestanding building constructed with a Whirlwind Steel Building system, the studio is a single space, sixty-four feet, three inches long on its north and south sides, fifty feet, three-and-an-eighth inches wide on its east and west fronts. Lundy doubled the eight-foot bay spacing he used for his wife's studio to arrive at sixteen-foot-wide bays. Here the mainframe beams span the length of the building. Lundy repeated the earlier studio's internal vertical stacking with

a solid wall rising twelve feet on the north side to the sill line of a six-foot-tall clerestory window. A two-foot-tall clerestory window spans the entire south wall. On the east and west sides, tall window and door openings are slotted into end bays. The studio's roof plane is ever so slightly tilted: the east-facing entrance wall rises eighteen feet, eight inches; the rear (west) wall rises twenty feet.

Lundy built his studio on a "flagpole" lot, Houston real estate slang for the rear parcel of a lot that has been split in two, with a sliver of property wide enough for a driveway running along one of the side property lines to connect to the street. The studio is located in the Gulfton corridor, a patchwork of garden apartment complexes, warehouses, and light industrial operations all jumbled together, attesting to Houston's status as the only major city in the United States without a zoning ordinance. Lundy's studio blends into this landscape, in part because it lies on the back of the subdivided lot, but also because it is surfaced, like many of the shed buildings in the Gulfton corridor, with low-rib, reversed Galvalume steel sheet siding. What distinguishes Lundy's studio is its precision. Internally the steel mainframe and the secondary structure of horizontal C-channels are exposed. The interior wall surface consists of vinyl-backed insulation installed within the interstices of the structural grid, held in place by vertical girts. It is when you notice that the girts overlapping the C-channels in the lower walls form square panels that you become aware of the deliberation with which Lundy deployed this standardized steel construction system. Steel X-bracing introduces floor-to-ceiling diagonals that visually activate this grid by emphasizing its graduated proportions. The six-foot-high window band on the north brings skylight, clouds, and the canopies of adjacent trees into the lofty interior. As in the Mulberry Lane art studio, Lundy introduced a freestanding "island" atop the polished concrete floor slab to contain plumbing, mechanical equipment, and storage spaces. Nothing is precious in the studio. Everything is exact, thoughtful, even witty. A north-facing door is surfaced with Galvalume so that it blends into the exterior wall surface when shut. The south-facing horizontal slot window is, of course, not parallel to the tilted roof above, introducing a hint of visual tension as you wonder if it looks out of whack just because you are seeing it at a funny angle (fig. 7).

Fig. 7 Lundy Studio, Houston, Texas, looking west, 1998, photographed in 2017

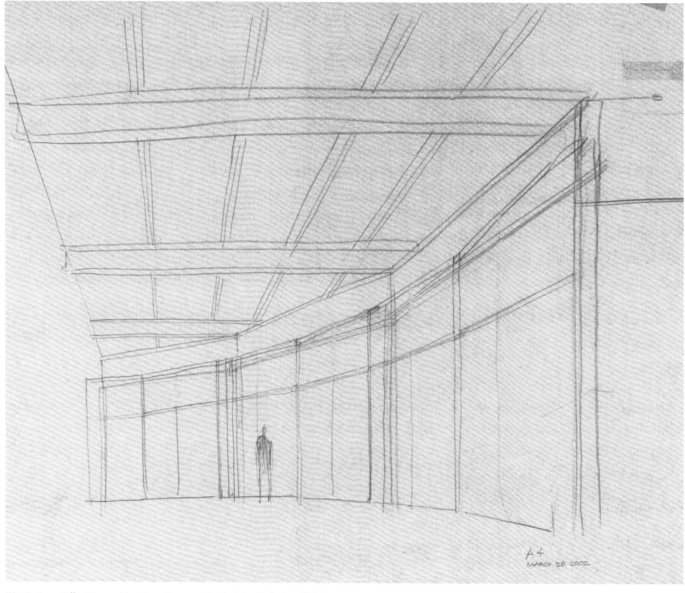

Fig. 8 Joan Miller House, Houston, Texas, early sketch of interior, 2002

Lundy's fourth Houston building, a house for Joan B. Miller, is located in Brunner, a turn-of-the-twentieth-century working-class neighborhood in the West End. In 1974 Fredericka Hunter, a Houston art dealer, and Simone Swan, executive vice president of the Menil Foundation, built two attached houses in the West End designed by Hunter's brother-in-law, the architect Eugene Aubry. To make the houses recede into the neighborhood of wood cottages interspersed with pre-engineered steel warehouse buildings, Aubry surfaced their walls and roofs with corrugated galvanized sheet iron, the material he and Howard Barnstone first applied at the Rice Museum and Media Center at Rice University in

1969–70. Fifteen years after the construction of what Hunter humorously nicknamed the "tin houses," young Houston architects—Natalye Appel, Cameron Armstrong, Val Glitsch, Rob Civitello, Donna Kacmar—launched the Tin House movement in the West End, designing economical houses in the mixed-use, mixed-race, mixed-income neighborhood for art collectors, dealers, artists, and architects. The young architects affiliated their houses with the original Tin Houses by cladding them with Galvalume. This marked the first time that Houston architects had extrapolated an architecture from the locale where their new buildings were built. Lundy's house for Miller is affiliated with the Tin

Fig. 9 Joan Miller House, Houston, Texas, early sketch of exterior, 2002

Houses through his use of the Whirlwind Steel Building system and exterior surfaces clad in Galvalume.

Lundy's journals, notes, and drawings document the stages through which the design evolved (figs. 8–9). Economy was a major concern, but so was his client's sensibility. The resulting design can be understood as a fusion of the Lundy House and Lundy's studio. The Miller House's spatial diagram is similar to that of the Lundy House. There is a street-facing garage with an entry that leads past the kitchen into the main space, which is oriented to the rear of the property. The Miller House differs in that it has a second-floor loft above a ground-floor bedroom and bathroom, and a separate dining room (now used as a sitting room) behind the garage. The house took form as a two-story shed buttressed by a one-story shed containing the garage.

Lundy translated the construction system of his studio to the Miller House. Not only is the house's galvanized steel frame exposed inside and out, the interior wall of the long, south-facing side wall is surfaced with vinyl-backed insulation sandwiched behind horizontal C-channels. (Miller uses one of the C-channels as a shelf to display works of art.) X-bracing accentuates one bay of this side wall, and the floor is the house's polished concrete foundation slab. The steel's

galvanized finish results in a brusque appearance that registers more strongly than in Lundy's studio. Lundy specified maple for the doors and kitchen cabinets, introducing a tonal and textural contrast that alleviates the prevailing gray of the other architectural surfaces.

These characteristics are strictly secondary, however. What stands out in the Miller House is the experience of entering the space. The living room ceiling is seventeen feet, ten inches high; the wall facing the rear courtyard is floor-to-ceiling glass, faceted in plan so that it curves to a point, intersecting the long south side wall at a sharp angle. When viewed in plan, the faceted wall gives the impression that space narrows down to an unusable point. But when you experience it in person, the glass wall exerts the opposite effect: it is as though the space turns gradually, beckoning you by stages to discover the courtyard, where old-growth trees shield the west-facing curtain wall from the setting sun. Miller's house is spectacular, and Lundy's orchestration of the space is exhilarating. Even the three-story townhouses, subsequently built next door, do not spoil the sensation of surprise and delight one feels upon entering the living room. If anything, they box in the Miller courtyard, defining it as an outdoor room that seems as lofty as the canopied interior of the living room.

As at his own house, Lundy did not expend all his design ingenuity on the big space. He intricately worked out the planning of the ground-floor bedroom and adjoining bath to maximize spatial economy through geometric reciprocity so that an opportune recess in one room becomes a clever, even necessary, projection in the adjoining space. Lundy's design of the stair exemplifies his spatial imagination. Leaving the underside of the stair open to the bedroom (rather than enclosing it and making it into a closet, for instance), he creates a deep, diagonally profiled spatial recess. This frames an interior structural column as well as the obscured glass corner window, illuminating the corner of the room with a pool of light and creating unprogrammed space that Miller accentuated with her placement of furniture.

Lundy's sketch notebooks show how he wrestled with the planning of these spaces to ensure what now seems like their inevitable congruence. Lundy took advantage of the house's variable roof heights to install a clerestory band that runs above the garage roofline and into the living room, beckoning arriving visitors to follow its fan-like unfolding as they traverse the entrance hall and move into the living room. By bringing northern sidelight into the house through this clerestory, Lundy creates the sensation, as at his own house, that the building fabric dissolves, bringing light, sky, and the surrounding tree canopies into the interior. Lundy stationed a tall, glazed opening rising the full height of the kitchen–living room on the cross-axis of the one-story sitting room, so that one moves through the space on an axis, not of symmetry, but of light.

The compartmentalized street front of the Miller House is more complex than that of the Lundy House. The tall glazed openings frame the central panel of Galvalume on the two-story bar, imbuing the house with a sense of fragility that is emphasized by the use of obscured glass. The height of the front door introduces an unexpected note of monumentality to the front elevation, hinting at the loftiness and grandeur of the interior but qualified immediately outside by the mottled, no-nonsense texture of the galvanized corner column. The wide eaves of the sloped roof plate give the top of the house a more emphatic presence than at Victor Lundy's house or studio. The juxtaposition of the house's countersloped roofs produces visual tension, charging the purposefully anonymous street front with an imbalance that is resolved not through compositional complacence but through the experience of the house's internal space (figs. 10–13).

The Miller House, the Lundy Studio, and the Lundy House and Studio exhibit the skill and assurance with which Victor Lundy continued to produce architecture throughout his career. This combination of few buildings and exceptionally high quality is paralleled in the work of two Houston architects of Lundy's generation, John Zemanek (1921–2016) and Anderson Todd (b. 1921).[2] Each architect's work is quite different. But Zemanek and Todd, like Lundy, combined conceptual ingenuity, fluid spatial imagination, and tectonic rigor to produce buildings that astound with their integrity. Lundy's Houston buildings reveal how the modernist ethos of economy, clarity, and rigor continues to inspire his architecture, leading him to produce masterworks that are no less rewarding for being small in size and few in number. The fertility of Lundy's spatial imagination, his extraordinary ability to translate ideas into drawings and buildings, and the consistency with which he conceives and executes designs ensure that each building he produces radiates an authority and precision that affects those who experience it. Friends of Anstis and Victor Lundy fondly recall the joyfulness, fun, and style with which they entertained on Mulberry Lane. Their love of life is a quality that Lundy has managed to impart to construction and space, and it is love of life that suffuses his buildings with powerful sensations of conviviality.

Fig. 10 (previous spread) Joan Miller House, looking northeast, 2003, photographed in 2017
Fig. 11 (opposite, top) Joan Miller House, view of kitchen, looking east, 2003, photographed in 2017
Fig. 12 (opposite, bottom) Joan Miller House, front facade, 2003, photographed in 2017
Fig. 13 (following spread) Joan Miller House, back facade, 2003, photographed in 2017

Sculpting Space

Donna Kacmar

The work of Victor Lundy can be organized many ways—by the date it was designed and built, the location of the work, or the type of building. However, some aspects of his work remain constant regardless of date, location, or type. The GSA-produced 2014 documentary film on Lundy's work describes him as a "sculptor of space." He truly is an artist, working with material substance and weight, as well as the more ephemeral qualities of light, to make space that befits the client's aspirations. His self-proclaimed "intuitive" design skills are informed by this interest in materials, deep understanding of structural forces, and close study of the behavior of light. Lundy continuously focused on how architectural form is enhanced by thoughtful use of materials, structural systems, and the movement of light in space.

After the technological advancements brought about during World War II, many architects explored newly developed materials, such as plywood, laminated wood, and plastic, in their work. Lundy differed from other contemporary architects by finding innovative applications for both new and traditional materials. He began probing materials early in his career and frequently commented on materiality in his journals and other writings as he searched for building solutions. Even in an early travel diary he notes "recipes"

for both timeless plaster and black polished floors.[1] Lundy also wrote on the importance of wood and concrete, as he sought to understand each material's nature, limitations, and opportunities.

He began using large, laminated-wood structures in his first buildings in Sarasota, including in the Sarasota County Chamber of Commerce building, Bee Ridge Presbyterian Church, St. Paul's Fellowship Hall, and Galloway's Furniture Showroom.[2] Lundy even used six laminated pine arches in a residential project, the Herron House, in Venice, Florida. He worked almost exclusively with Timber Structures, Inc. from Portland, Oregon, often drawing the shape he envisioned, full scale, on the floor of their workshop. He continued using laminated-wood structures in later projects while exploring smaller linear wood elements in projects such as the I. Miller Showroom, the Singer Showroom, and the shade structures for the Smithsonian.[3]

Construction on the I. Miller Showroom, at the corner of Fifth Avenue and Fifty-Seventh Street in New York City, started in March 1961 and was completed one year later (fig. 1). Lundy cut through three structural bays on the second floor to make a thirty-five-foot-tall entry space, wrapped by a mezzanine above. He then created a "wood curtain" and, "in one stroke, starting at the top of the

Fig. 1 I. Miller Showroom, New York City, Great Hall, 1962

Fig. 2 I. Miller Showroom, New York City, Great Hall, 1962

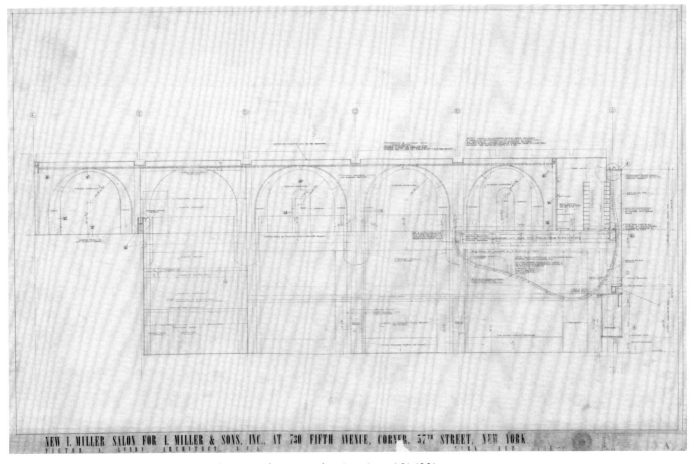

Fig. 3 I. Miller Showroom, New York City, north interior elevation and section, August 31, 1961

exterior, swept it past the limited perimeter beam then down under, lowering the scale of the street level selling space at the perimeter and sweeping it upward to culminate in a railing for the mezzanine."[4] John Gallin & Son, Inc., the general contractor, looked to Timber Structures for the fabrication and erection of the laminated fire-treated wood for the 14,600-square-foot interior.

The dramatic entry is hinted at through the large glass window along the mostly stone facade facing Fifth Avenue (fig. 2). Visitors enter a low, intimate L-shaped area before stepping into the expanded space (fig. 3). The large curving entry wall extends throughout the space and ends at the railing on the mezzanine floor, creating one continuous two-story surface. Lundy recollects, "It is make-believe… fun. It was created out of nothingness. Commercial interiors, it seems to me, are a make-believe process. Don't take it too seriously, just go in and enjoy it."[5]

The showroom's existing structural columns were encased in curved laminated hemlock strips, and the continuous surface was actually made from individual sections of hemlock that were interwoven to create the uniform surface[6] (fig. 4). Mirrored surfaces, inserted between wood slats, reflect the wood and the space back to the viewer, making "the space burst its boundaries."[7]

As Lundy wrote in the 1962 American Institute of Architects (AIA) entry submission text, "This is more than an interior. It demonstrates the possibility of creating a total and serious new architectural environment that reaches in a high dimension out of existing spaces and volumes (of an existing building)." His intention was "to create beauty, in an abundant, luxurious atmosphere." Sadly, in 1991, he received a phone call "out of the blue" from New York City that Bulgari was now leasing the I. Miller space and taking down the entire exuberant wood interior of the showroom. Lundy

(continued on page 196)

Fig. 4 Fabrication of column for I. Miller Showroom at Timber Structures (timber fabrication company), Portland, Oregon, 1961
Fig. 5 (opposite) I. Miller Showroom, New York City, Grand Hall from above, 1962
Fig. 6 (following spread) I. Miller Showroom, New York City, ceiling detail, 1962

Fig. 7 (opposite) I. Miller Showroom, New York City, corner column, 1962
Fig. 8 (above) I. Miller Showroom, New York City, ceiling at Grand Hall, 1962

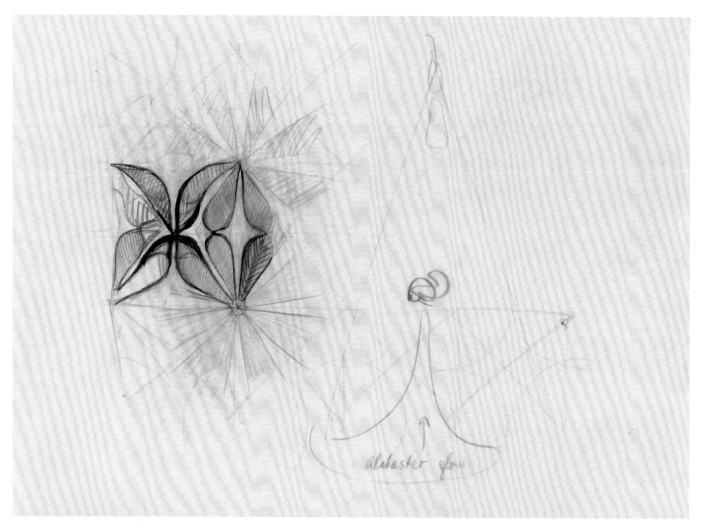

Fig. 9 Singer Showroom, New York City, sketch of petal, 1964. Graphite on tracing paper, 43 x 36 inches
Fig. 10 Singer Showroom sketch, New York City, 1964

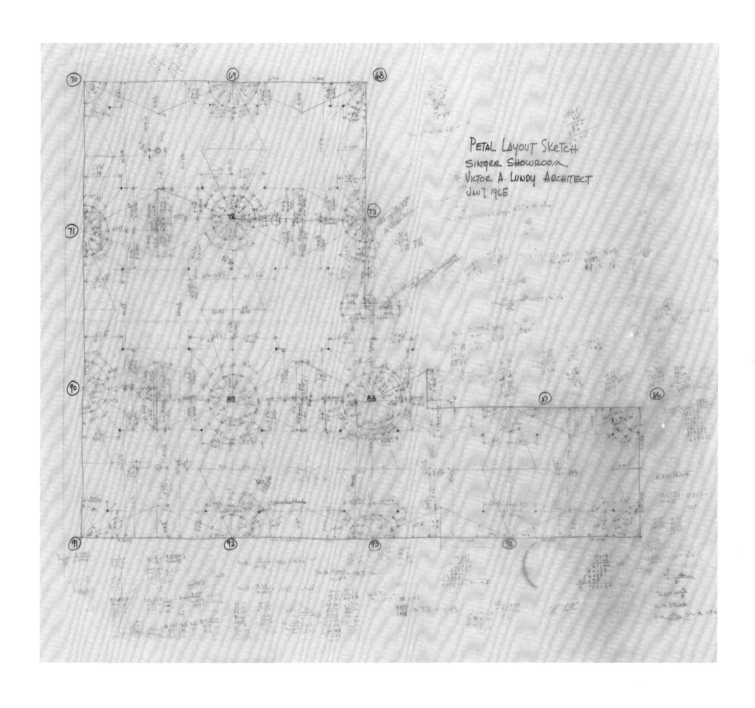

Fig. 11 Singer Showroom, New York City, petal layout sketch, July 1964
Fig. 12 (following spread) Singer Showroom, New York City, 1965

Fig. 13 (opposite) Singer Showroom, New York City, column detail, 1965
Fig. 14 (above) Singer Showroom gallery, New York City, 1965

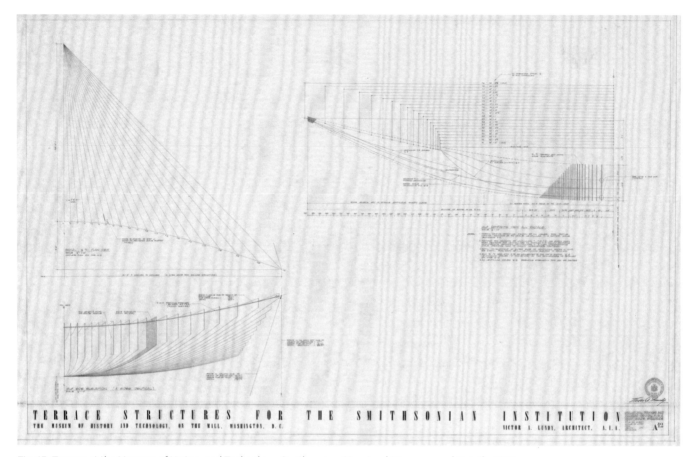

Fig. 15 Terrace at the Museum of History and Technology, Smithsonian, Structural Diagrams and Details, 1965
Fig. 16 (opposite) Shade structure, Smithsonian Institution, Museum of History and Technology, Washington, DC, 1965

returned the call, but he was too late to save the sumptuous interior (figs. 5–8).

In 1964 Lundy designed the Singer Showroom at Rockefeller Center, also in New York City[8] (figs. 9–10). The first floor contains an L-shaped sales area and the lower level houses an art gallery. He again used clear hemlock strips to create wooden "petals" that wrap each column and are set against a curved plaster ceiling.[9] Japanese grass-cloth wallpaper and bronze detailing complete the material palette. Mirrors on the back walls extend the space to the street and "make the luminous pavilion seem to extend through the whole street level of the building."[10]

The interior space is dominated by the structural columns wrapped with wooden petals. The petals' sizing was governed by the diameter of the largest column in the basement, which determined the face of the wall and radius of the petals (fig. 11). In all, there are sixty-seven different petal configurations, some up to nine feet wide, and most

almost five feet wide. Cables, connected to a point eighteen inches from each petal end, are in turn attached to the structure above, with horizontal stiffeners every two feet. Each petal has vertical strips applied to its face and narrow wood strips wrap around each edge. Another series of continuous wood strips curves from the ceiling down the face of each petal, articulating the form. Lundy even aligned the orientation of the carpet patterns with the wood strips of the ceiling above. The artificial lighting scheme was also studied: glass rod down-lights by Venini Glass are distributed in areas of intensity (figs. 12–14).

Lundy also used small linear wood elements to design the shade structures at the Smithsonian Museum of Natural History in Washington, DC, in 1965. He designed three suspended squares, each composed of a series of three-quarter-inch square strips of western red cedar, all of varying lengths, hung on cable in concentric circles. The space between the wooden strips allows breezes to flow through,

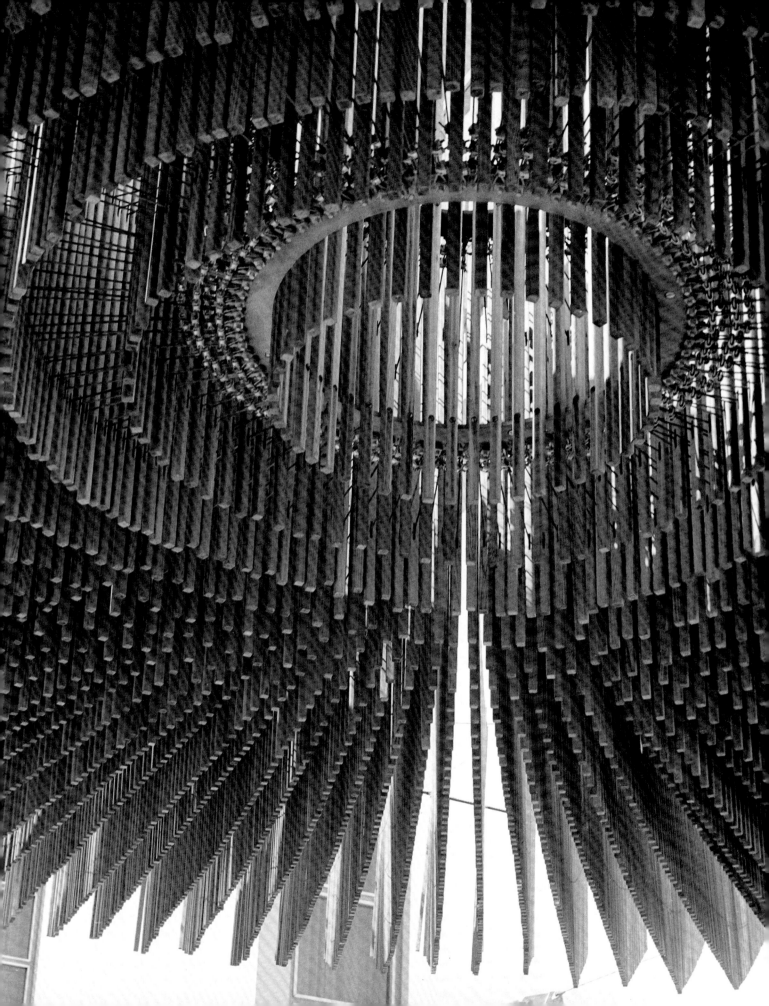

creating a cool, shaded patio below (figs. 15–18). Lundy continued to develop thin wood elements for many of his buildings, including the hanging wooden ceiling at Hartford Unitarian Church and the wood ceiling and grilles at the US Tax Court Building (fig. 19). The wood details and sunscreens at the US Embassy in Sri Lanka are also part of this tradition.

Lundy also explored other materials in his buildings, including reinforced concrete and masonry. In the IBM Garden State Office Building in Cranford, New Jersey, Lundy explored both of these materials. His use of reinforced concrete was informed by his understanding of wood—this time translated into fiberglass formwork. The IBM Corporation, under a program directed by architect Eliot Noyes, hired world-class architects to design its regional office buildings in the 1960s. The prescribed program of 43,000 square feet did not give Lundy much to work with. He grouped the sales force in the central space to make the workplace of those who travel, or "go out" into the world, to work something special. In this central space, each of the ten-inch-diameter columns flare to the tree-shaped capital and floor slab above (fig. 20). The reusable forms, made from glass-fiber reinforced polyester resin, were molded from wood strip originals, with each rib spaced one and a half inches apart. A special four-thousand-psi concrete mix, with maximum aggregate size limited to three-eighths of an inch, forms the vertical cantilevered columns and thin shell roof.[11] Each of the twenty-two-foot square "trees" changes its height in relationship to exterior walls, creating a forested courtyard inside the office building. A playful masonry exterior, made by using several templates, recalls the ruins of the Uxmal pyramid in Mexico, with the reverse pattern on the interior walls[12] (fig. 21). Earlier examples of Lundy's expressive masonry include the textured walls, enlivened by sun-cast shadows, at Bee Ridge Presbyterian Church and the Alta Vista Elementary School addition. Given the limited budgets of most of Lundy's buildings, each material needed to be used efficiently and effectively. Lundy extracted the most textural and formal content he could from materials, resulting in unusual pairings of clarity and surprise.

Structural innovation has always been essential to Lundy's work. Throughout his career, he collaborated with highly qualified structural engineers while developing his own understanding of structural behavior.[13] This interest was evident in all his churches, especially the early ones in Sarasota. As architecture critic Richard Ingersoll notes, "Lundy's structurally innovative concrete and Glulam beam construction for churches in the area still seems astoundingly original."[14]

One of Lundy's structural innovations involved a new form of space making using inflatable structures known as pneumatics. Lundy found an overlap between form, efficiency, and constructability in both his traveling exhibition hall for the US Atomic Energy Commission and his "space flowers" for the Brass Rail restroom and refreshment stands at the World's Fair (1964–65).

In 1960 the Atomic Energy Commission (AEC) asked Lundy to design an exhibition building that could be moved to various cities in South America as part of the US Atoms for Peace program. He collaborated with Walter Bird from Birdair Structures, Inc. to design a structure for a twenty-two-thousand-square-foot building that would house a theater, exhibit, and technical space (fig. 25). In the awards entry Lundy writes, "I wanted it to be a sassy, unafraid example of US ingenuity."[15]

The selection of the structural system was based on portability, high structural efficiency, safety, ease of field service and repair, and ease of erection. Wood structures, steel lamella roofs, Kaiser aluminum domes, and an aluminum tent were all considered. Lundy also did not want an overly complicated and detailed building that might compete with the exhibits inside. He wanted to "create a total environment where the exhibit itself takes over"[16] (fig. 22). After considerable correspondence with Bird and review of extensive technical data and information, Lundy selected a pneumatic structural system in April 1960.[17] Blue lights and bright exhibits illuminate the interior space. Outside "it resembled a puffed-up Henry Moore sculpture."[18] Lundy jokes that the inspiration for the building shape was his wife lying on her side on a beach (figs. 23–27).

The inflatable structure is composed of two vinyl-coated nylon skins with a four-foot air space and eight chambers between the layers. Continuous rated centrifugal blowers provide inflation pressure and a rigid end-frame at both ends.

(continued on page 209)

Fig. 17 Shade structure, Smithsonian Institution, Museum of History and Technology, Washington, DC, detail, 1965

Fig. 18 (previous spread) Shade Structure, Smithsonian Institution, Museum of History and Technology, Washington, DC, side view, 1965
Fig. 19 (above) Hartford Unitarian Church, Hartford, Connecticut, with wood ceiling under construction, 1964

Fig. 20 IBM Garden State Office Building, Cranford, New Jersey, 1964

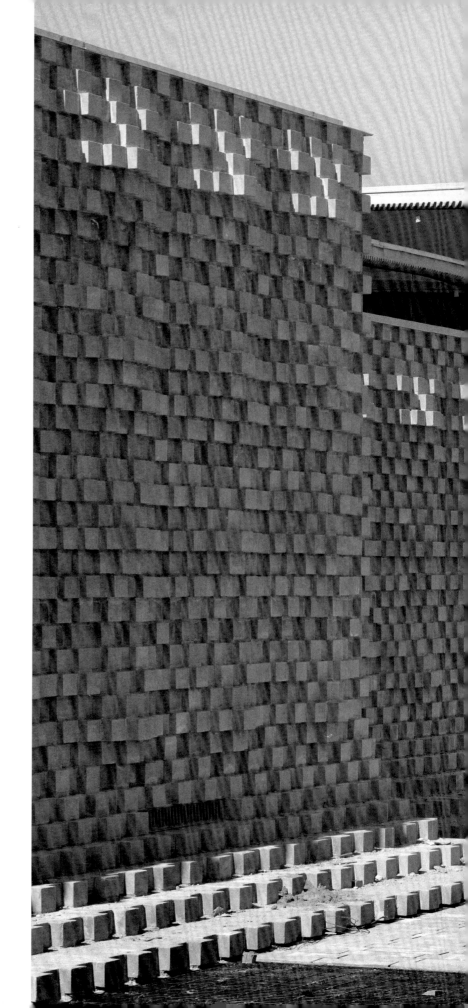

Fig. 21 IBM Garden State Office Building, Cranford, New Jersey, exterior masonry wall, 1964

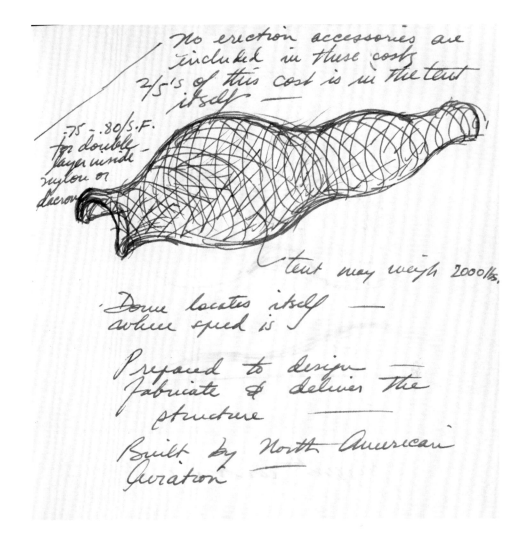

Fig. 22 (opposite, top) Atomic Energy Commission exhibit rendering, 1960

Fig. 23 (opposite, bottom) Atomic Energy Commission exhibition rendering, 1960

Fig. 24 (top) Atomic Energy Commission (AEC) exhibit, sketch from Lundy's 1960 AEC brains book, 1960

Fig. 25 (bottom) Atomic Energy Commission exhibition, Rio de Janeiro, Brazil, 1961

Fig. 26 (top) Atomic Energy Commission exhibition, Buenos Aires, Argentina, 1960
Fig. 27 (bottom) Atomic Energy Commission exhibition, Buenos Aires, Argentina, 1960

The entire building was 300 feet long, with a maximum width of 126 feet and maximum height of 53.5 feet, yet it weighed only twenty-eight tons (less than five ounces per square foot) and could be packed into just five thousand cubic feet for shipping.[19] The building took four days to erect, using just twelve laborers.[20]

The building was efficiently designed at a cost of $99,870, with about $25,000 required for site work in each city. The exhibit opened in November 1960 in Buenos Aires and then traveled to Rio de Janeiro, Lima, Santiago, and Montevideo, before arriving in Mexico City in April 1962.[21] The structure was refurbished and then went on an extended tour to Dublin, Ankara, Tehran, Baghdad, and Tunis. The project was published in *Americas*, *Architectural Forum*, *Building Research: Journal of the BRAB Building Research Institute*, *Nuestra arquitectura*, *Metals & Controls*, and *Time* magazine, and it won a Silver Medal for Engineering from the Architectural League of New York.

Lundy returned to pneumatic structures in his space flowers for the New York World's Fair in 1964 and 1965. Brass Rail Restaurant, which was providing the restrooms and refreshment stands at the fair, contacted him, and after the first interview, Lundy traveled with the restaurant's president and his son to Denmark to tour the Carlsberg beer factory and taste the beer that would be served at the stands.[22] Lundy designed the restrooms and public counters for ordering, and the tables, chairs, and signage. He had fallen in love with the efficiency of the air-supported structures during the atomic energy exhibit and decided to use them again at the fair. Starting with a clay model to develop his original concept, he worked again with Birdair to later reduce the number of curved sections and fabric size to gain efficiency (figs. 30–32). Segmented fabric forms a globe shape that floats to a height of seventy-five feet, soaring above the crowds and providing shelter to those below. When illuminated at night, the inflated fabric panels transmit light and serve as beacons. From below, they appear as flowers suspended in space, with the stitches and fabric joinery throwing patterns onto the surfaces underneath (figs. 33–37). When the flowers were completed, Lundy received a call from Philip Johnson, who asked, "What have you done?" He added, "We are all wild about them."[23]

Lundy continued this interest in pneumatic structures for several years. He was invited by Frei Otto to present a technical paper on his air-supported structures in Stuttgart, West Germany, at an international conference in May 1967.[24]

Structure is clearly expressed in most of Lundy's buildings. The Warm Mineral Springs Motel, with its seventy-five hyperbolic parabolas that were each cast on the ground before being lifted to become concrete umbrellas, explored thin-shell concrete structures. Perhaps his most sophisticated and inventive structure is in the sanctuary of St. Paul's Lutheran Church in Sarasota. He worked with Severud Associates and the structural engineers Dr. Ziev and Hannskarl Bandel to develop a system for the roof that clearly shows tensile forces. Custom steel brackets, spaced every eight feet, form a steel truss that connects to hanging steel cables. Steel is post-tensioned on the bottom of the truss, forming one element that acts like a beam to span from the altar to the front of the church.[25] At the US Tax Court Building in Washington, DC, Lundy used concrete double T's for most of the building structure, and an impressive fifty-five-foot cantilever, anchored by numerous tension cables, supports the courtrooms that hover over visitors as they ascend the front stairs. Lundy again worked with Severud Associates to develop a structural system that rivals St. Paul's sanctuary in its sophistication.[26]

Lundy choreographs the play of light to help inform space. In his Beaux-Arts training, light was an important ingredient in the painting and drawing. The importance of light in his renderings became realized in each of his buildings. Lundy readily admits that in his earlier buildings it was about bringing in as much natural light as possible until he "discovered the magic of controlling it."[27] In his religious buildings, he often used light in mysterious and innovative ways to bring focus to the altar. In the East Harlem Church, the only natural light came from the skylight above the altar. In the Westport Unitarian Church, light filters from the space between the two soaring wings via a skylight that runs the length of the roof ridge, helping the roof appear to float above parishioners gathered below. Light is also used to draw the congregation toward the altar or other point of focus.

Lundy uses light to animate circulation spaces in secular buildings, often emphasizing the entry area. In the US Tax Court Building, daylight washes into the multistory atrium and grand hall. In Intermediate School 53 in Queens, New York, the atrium in the entry space is light filled, vertical fins create shade and shadow that play throughout circulation corridors, and each classroom has a skylight that washes the walls (figs. 28–29). In the US Embassy in Sri Lanka, a series

Fig. 28 Intermediate School 53, atrium, Queens, New York, 1973

Fig. 29 Intermediate School 53, hallway, Queens, New York, 1973

of light wells extends down through the floor, bringing natural light into the central hallway that feeds each office.

Lundy also uses natural light to direct focus in smaller buildings. In his own house in Bellaire, a large skylight, augmented with artificial lighting for dramatic nighttime viewing, directs bright light above the grand fireplace. Similarly, the oversized fireplace in the Lundys' Aspen house is drenched with light from above and each side, emphasizing the solidity of the masonry element against the thin glass membranes immediately adjacent to it.

A similar attitude is taken with artificial lighting. In the Tax Court Building, private galleries that serve the judges' offices are edged with lighting that illuminates a sidewall of the passageways. In Lundy's buildings, the location of light fixtures coordinates with structural elements to form patterns, emphasize circulation, or highlight changes of materials. Lundy designed buildings to share a consistent handling of both natural and artificial light that is recognizable upon entry.

Lundy's work shows his skillful handling of material, structure, and light, focusing on the timeless quality of space making in architecture. His work realizes a unique union of respect for traditional modes and modern intentions. Lundy's place in modern architecture is singular. His

work, informed by modernist tenets of utility and abstraction, embraces a timeless humanity and spirit. Lundy, an architect and an artist, uses his innate drawing skill, understanding of materials and structural behavior, and manipulation of light in direct service to his art form. His son, Nicholas Lundy, agrees:

> He is a Modernist, but more importantly, thoroughly modern. His buildings have a kind of elegant serenity about them, and our shared joke has been that no one would ever use the word "serene" to describe him personally. But "elegant" yes, in his own way, certainly in the quality of his intellect and approach to his work. His buildings are perfect in their proportion and sense of scale, so too his drawings. The ability to communicate a three-dimensional idea straight through his hand onto a piece of paper with seemingly no effort is a profound gift and one that I think he was born with. My father used to say that one aspired to make art, and to be an artist was a calling. An "artist" is not a vague, self-congratulatory term one throws out about oneself. It is a title to be earned and bestowed. So I'll say it…my father, in every fiber of his being, is an artist.[28]

Fig. 30 Space Flowers, New York World's Fair, Flushing Meadows, New York, drawing of cross section, May 20, 1963
Fig. 31 Space Flowers, New York World's Fair, Flushing Meadows, New York, sketch, 1963

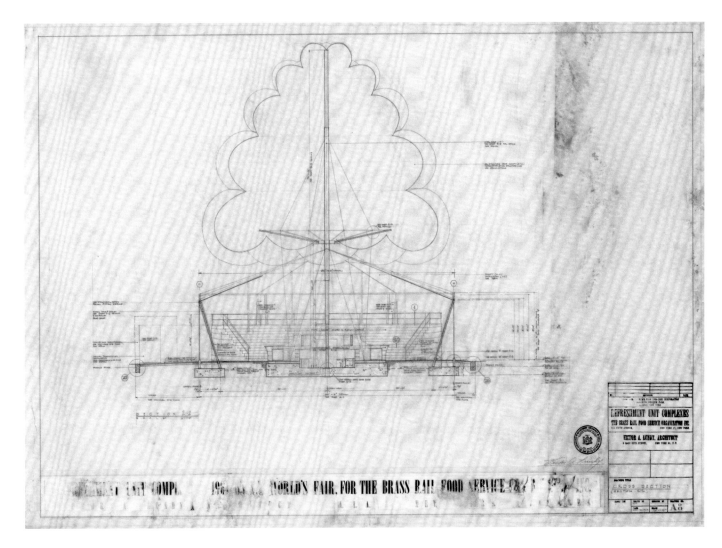

Fig. 32 Space Flowers, New York World's Fair, sketch, 1963
Fig. 33 (right) Space Flowers, New York World's Fair, 1964

Fig. 34 Space Flowers, New York World's Fair, 1964
Fig. 35 (right) Space Flowers, New York World's Fair, 1964

Fig. 36 Space Flowers, New York World's Fair, 1964
Fig. 37 (right) Space Flowers, New York World's Fair, 1964

Notes

Preface

1. Nicholas Lundy, note to author, May 17, 2017.
2. Victor Lundy, *Beyond the Harvard Box* (2006).

The Life and Work of Victor Lundy

1. Victor Lundy, interview by author, Bellaire, TX, March 7, 2016.
2. Ibid.
3. Victor Lundy, interview by author, Bellaire, TX, May 24, 2017.
4. Victor Lundy, interview by author, Bellaire, TX, March 7, 2016
5. Ibid.
6. Victor Lundy, interview by author, Bellaire, TX, December 17, 2015, March 7, 2016, and March 28, 2016.
7. Victor Lundy, interview by author, Bellaire, TX, April 11, 2016.
8. Victor Lundy, interview by author, Bellaire, TX, March 28, 2016.
9. Victor Lundy, interview by author, Bellaire, TX, December 17, 2015, March 7, 2016, and March 28, 2016.
10. Lundy, interview by author, April 11, 2016.
11. Ibid.
12. Ibid.
13. Ibid.
14. Ibid.
15. Lundy was awarded the Rotch scholarship on the second try. On his first submission, the Rotch was awarded to Dale Bird. Lundy was encouraged to apply again. On Lundy's second submission, he beat out Paul Rudolph.
16. Victor Lundy, interview by author, Bellaire, TX, November 14, 2017.
17. Victor Lundy, note dated February 20, 1961, in "Brains Book," Container A263, Victor Lundy Archives, Library of Congress.
18. The passengers in the car are Victor and Shirley and their daughter.
19. Pierlugi Serraino, *The Creative Architect: Inside the Great Midcentury Personality Study* (New York: Monacelli, 2016).

20. Boyd Blackner, written description printed in *The Sarasota School of Architecture: 1941–1966*, by John Howey (Cambridge, MA: MIT Press, 1994), 109.
21. *United States Department of State Feasibility Study and Report for the United States Embassy Office Building*, Colombo, Sri Lanka, August 18, 1976, Victor Lundy Archives, Library of Congress.
22. Victor Lundy, lecture, Ball State University, October 30, 1972, libx.bsu.edu/cdm/singleitem/collection/CAPLectures/id/35/rec/2.
23. Comments from video, www.youtube.com/watch?v=s6umLipF7-E.
24. Bryan Trubey, phone conversation with author, April 3, 2017.
25. James Atkins, interview by author, Dallas, TX, July 18, 2017.
26. Ibid.

Artist Architect

1. See Prints and Photographs Division Online Catalog (PPOC): Victor A. Lundy Archive, PR 13 CN 2008:090, www.loc.gov/pictures/item/2010650114/.
2. For information concerning Lundy's early aptitude for drawing and education, see Donna Kacmar's "The Life and Works of Victor Lundy."
3. "N.Y.U. Will Confer Architect's Degree," *New York Times*, May 27, 1928. The advisory board then included a number of New York's leading architects: Chester H. Aldrich of Delano & Aldrich, Raymond Hood, C. Grant LaFarge, Benjamin Wistar Morris, Kenneth Murchison, and Charles C. Zantzinger, among others.
4. "Designers to Lecture at N.Y.U.," *New York Times*, September 1, 1940: "10 of the outstanding industrial designers of the country will lecture this Fall at the New York University School of Architecture and Allied Arts."
5. "Architects Study Here by Paris Method," *New York Times*, September 8, 1929: "Professor says N.Y.U. Courses are like those at Ecole des Beaux-Arts."

6. See "World War II Sketches by Victor A. Lundy," with an overview of his eight surviving sketchbooks from that time, containing 159 drawings, LOT 14007 (H) [P&P], www.loc.gov/rr/print/coll/628_lundy.html, with a link to a transcription of an interview with Lundy: Tracy A. Sugarman, World War II drawings in "Experiencing War," Veterans History Project, Library of Congress, lcweb2.loc.gov/diglib/vhp/story/loc.natlib.afc2001001.05440/. For additional information about Lundy's WWII experiences, see Kacmar's introduction.
7. For a description and contemporary photograph of Breuer's original residence, see "Breuer House I, New Canaan," last edited by Bostjan, March 16, 2016, accessed August 25, 2017, architectuul.com/architecture/breuer-house-i-new-canaan.
8. Donna Kacmar, Chronological Reconstruction of Victor Lundy's Itinerary during his Rotch Travelling Scholarship, 1948–1950, based upon his correspondence with and reports to the Boston Society of Architects. For additional information concerning Lundy's Rotch Scholarship, see Kacmar's "The Life and Works of Victor Lundy."
9. Victor Lundy, interview by Donna Kacmar, Bellaire, TX, August 2017.
10. For an excellent description of the role of drawing and the working methods of the Lundy office in Sarasota, see the account given by Lundy's draftsman during that period, Boyd Blackner, in Kacmar's "The Life and Works of Victor Lundy."
11. See also a discussion of the Sarasota Chamber of Commerce building, the "The Pagoda Building," in Christopher Wilson's essay in "The Sarasota Years."
12. Compare with Christopher Domin's illustrations of Lundy's 1959 renderings for the First Unitarian Church in Westport, Connecticut, also done on brown paper (page 103, figs. 13–14).

13. See Lundy, interviews with Donna Kacmar, where he explained his technique and purposes in the use of Wolff's Carbon Pencils and charcoal. Examples of Lundy's working drawings and his sketches, preliminary, and presentation drawings can be seen in the illustrations in other chapters: page 20, fig. 6; page 56, fig. 4; page 69, fig. 13; pages 78–80, fig. 21–22; page 92, fig. 4; page 108–10, fig. 18–22; page 120, fig. 30; page 130, fig. 2; pages 131–33, figs. 3–7; pages 149–51, figs. 2–5; page 165, fig. 3; pages 172–73, figs. 8–9; page 206, figs. 22–23.

14. Lundy, interviews with Donna Kacmar.

15. Ballroom Marfa, *The Art and Architecture of Anstis and Victor Lundy*, 2006.

16. See Domin's discussion of the sanctuary of St. Paul's Lutheran Church, which quotes Lundy's own description of his architectural and artistic intentions, in "Sacred Spaces."

17. See the photograph by George Cserna showing a similar view of the sanctuary of St. Paul's Lutheran Church, also a likely inspiration for Lundy's rendering (page 123, fig. 33).

18. Compare with illustrations of Lundy's initial sketches for the US Tax Court Building in Joan Brierton's discussion of the same (pages 130–35, figs. 2–8).

19. Lundy, interviews with Donna Kacmar.

20. "Greg Lynn: Organic Algorithms in Architecture | TED Talk," image.slidesharecdn.com/animateform-redo-120620045932-phpapp02/95/animateform-26-728.jpg?cb=1340280111 and www.ted.com/talks/greg_lynn_on_organic_design (accessed August 25, 2017).

21. About 1960 Lundy began to employ Cray-Pas (an abbreviation of "crayon" and "pastel") oil pastels in his drawings, especially in his travel drawings and sketches and in his "brains books." The medium was first developed in the 1920s, and Lundy confirmed in an August 2017 interview with Donna Kacmar, based on the author's queries, that through the years he used the Japanese Sakura brand exclusively.

22. Lundy, interviews with Donna Kacmar.

23. Ibid.

24. Ibid.

25. The Pantheon was another favorite subject that Lundy drew repeatedly and from many different points of view.

The Sarasota Years

1. Sarasota's population grew during this decade from nineteen thousand in 1950 to thirty-four thousand in 1960.

2. Sarasota writers in the 1950s included the mystery writer John MacDonald; the authors Duane Decker, Walter Farley, Mary Freeman, and Richard Glendinning; the novelists Mackinlay Kantor and Borden Deal; the screenwriter Budd Schulberg; the playwright Joseph Hayes; and the short story writer Wyat Blassingame. Painters included Mildred Adams, John Armstrong, Beth Arthur, Judy Shepherd Axe, Elsinore Budd, Jack Cartlidge, Robert Chase, Shirley Clement, Stella Coler, Fiore Custode, Julio de Diego, Sally Boyd Dillard, Truman Fassett, George Fox, Genevieve Hamel, Martha and William Hartman, George Kaiser, Robert Larson, Roy Nichols, Helen Frank Protas, Frank Rampolla, Eve Root, Elden Rowland, Craig Rubadoux, Guy Saunders, Helen Sawyer (referred to as "the heart of the Sarasota art world" in Jeff LaHurd, *Sarasota: A History* [Charleston, SC: History Press, 2006], 110), her husband, Wells Sawyer, Eric von Schmidt, Elsa Selian, Jan Silberstein, Harold Slingerland, Syd Solomon, Rose H. Spitzer, Lois Bartlett Tracy, and Betty Warren. Painting schools/studios were run by the artists Frank Swift Chase, Nancy Coldwell, Jerry Farnsworth, Irene M. Jensen, Hilton and Dorothy Leech, Laura Lock, and Helen Q. Remsen. Leslie Thomas Posey ran a sculpture school/studio. In addition to Ben Stahl, illustrators included Al Buell, Thornton Robyn Utz, and Al Parker. Musicians included Eddie Egars and Wilmer C. Banks. Photographers included Joseph Steinmetz and W. Earl Burnell. Steinmetz established a photography studio in Sarasota in 1941 and did quite well documenting the buildings of the "Sarasota School" architects Bert Brosmith, Joseph Farrell, Mark Hampton, Gene Leedy, Paul Rudolph, William Rupp, Tim Seibert, Ralph Twitchell, Jack West, and the father-and-son team of Ralph and William Zimmerman. Although not officially an architect, Philip H. Hiss, a prominent citizen of Sarasota and the developer of Lido Shores, is often included in this list because he sketched house designs that were then constructed by local builders. Hiss is also important because of his role in commissioning Sarasota School architects, especially as school board head between 1954 and 1960, and founding chairman of the Board of Trustees of New College, Sarasota, 1960. Ringling School of Art, opened in 1931, began to award four-year BFA degrees in 1979. In 2007 the institution changed its name to Ringling College of Art + Design. Ringling Museum, founded in 1927, was rebranded as "The Ringling" in 2013, reflecting the fact that the complex, run by Florida State University since 2000, consists of not only the art museum but also a library/educational center, circus museum, historic mansion (John and Mable Ringling's "Cà d'Zan"), eighteenth-century theater brought over piece by piece from Asolo, Italy (the Historic Asolo Theater), and expansive gardens and grounds.

3. See www.sarasotahistoryalive.com/history/articles/the-making-of-an-art-colony (accessed June 9, 2017).

4. The idea of a Sarasota School first appeared in a 1967 article in *Architectural Forum* by Philip Hiss, "Whatever Happened to Sarasota? (Sarasota's Broken Promise)" (vol. 126, no. 5). The architect Gene Leedy is given credit for inventing the moniker "Sarasota School of Architecture" at the 1982 AIA Florida convention in Tampa, titled "A Quest in Time: Sarasota Architecture Revisited." The principal speakers were listed as Paul Rudolph, Mark Hampton, Victor Lundy, and Gene Leedy, but Jack West, William Rupp, Bert Brosmith, and Tim Seibert also spoke. About the moniker "Sarasota School," Seibert has said, "We didn't call it that then….We just called it architecture" (www.heraldtribune.com/news/20171029/sarasota-mod-weekend-peoples-architect [accessed October 29, 2017]).

5. The other founding artists of the Famous Artists School were John Atherton, Austin Briggs, Stevan Dohanos, Albert Dorne, Robert Fawcett, Peter Helck, Fred Ludekens, Al Parker, Ben Stahl, Harold von Schmidt, and Jon Whitcomb. Knight and Lundy completed residences for Mr. and Mrs. Ingalls (East Aurora, NY, 1950), Robert and Agnes Fawcett (Ridgefield, NJ, 1953), and Ben and Ella Stahl (Sarasota, FL, 1954).

6. Marcia Jon Corbino, "Ben Stahl….At Work and at Home in Mexico," *Sarasota Herald-Tribune*, January 25, 1981.

7. The rectangular grid of the Stahl House was based on "the golden proportion" and measured about ten by sixteen feet. The house was published (credited only to Knight) in *HOUSE + HOME* magazine, May 1956, where the actual mathematical formula for the golden proportion was given ($a / b = b / a + b$). In an April 12, 2014, interview with the author, Lundy stated, "I felt entrapped….Those projects were all Reggie's." Interestingly, the entry for Victor A. Lundy in the 1956 AIA Directory of Architects lists "Previous Firm: Knight-Lundy Architects, Partnership, 1950–53," whereas the entry for Reginald Knight in the same edition does not list Knight-Lundy. Even more interesting, in the Lundy Archives at the Library of Congress

there is a drawing of a nondescript "Cottage for Mr. and Mrs. Stanley W. Brower, Plainfield, New Jersey," dated February 2, 1953, and sealed with a Knight-Lundy official State of New Jersey AIA stamp. From the lettering on the drawing, the author surmises that Lundy was responsible for it, hence the inclusion in his archive after more than sixty years.

8. In Sarasota Knight is credited with the Ben Stahl House on Siesta Key (1954), the John Shuler House on Longboat Key (ca. 1959), and a commercial building at 824 S. Osprey Avenue (1956). In Sarasota's northerly neighbor of Bradenton, he designed the Municipal Auditorium and the Manatee County Elementary School, a.k.a. New First Street School (both 1960). Elsewhere in Florida, Knight completed the First Baptist Church/Lake Shipp Chapel in Winter Haven (1958); College Park Education Building, Orlando (1955); First Federal Building, Cocoa Beach (1961, a controversial glass bank); and a hospital in Cape Canaveral (1961). In 1957 Knight was awarded first prize in the Enrico Fermi Memorial World Architectural Competition, to be located in Chicago. This memorial was never built, but has been described as "a one-story square block building with a glowing white roof for people to walk on while music emanates from forty-eight six-story chimney-like tubular bells" (*Chicago Tribune*, March 22, 1957).

9. See the documentary "An American Legacy: Sarasota School of Architecture," 36:32–36:50, produced and directed by Heather Dunhill and Bill Wagy, 2001, The [Sarasota] Fine Arts Society, sponsored in part by Comcast Cable Company and the Goldsmith-Greenfield Foundation, www.youtube.com/watch?v=h-CZX9dnOFM&t=2210s (accessed May 27, 2017).

10. "Drive-In Church: Floridians Worship in Cars," *Life* magazine, April 18, 1955, 175–78.

11. This project was called an "Ice-a-Teria" and was only eight by twenty-four feet.

12. This statement has most recently been repeated in the General Service Administration's 2014 documentary *Victor Lundy: Sculptor of Space*. See opening sequence, 0:00–0:09, www.youtube.com/watch?v=s6umLipF7-E (accessed May 31, 2017).

13. Karl Bickel (1882–1972) was originally from Geneseo, Illinois. He spent his career in the newspaper business, retiring as president of the United Press Association in 1935 and moving with his wife to Sarasota. Bickel was active in the city's development, leading efforts to build the Municipal Auditorium (1938) and

Lido Casino (1940), as well as being involved in decisions about housing, recreation facilities, highways, and hospitals. In 1960 he donated two parcels of land that became part of the New College campus.

14. Many subsequent buildings in Sarasota, particularly furniture stores on South Tamiami Trail, have adopted similar blue-tiled roofs, but since none of them use full-height glass walls, they are simply, in the words of Robert Venturi and Denise Scott-Brown, "decorated sheds." See architectureinsarasota.blogspot.com/2015/10/victor-lundy-and-ubiquity-of-blue.html (accessed June 1, 2017).

15. In 1994 Boyd Blackner, Lundy employee between 1959 and 1963, described to John Howey (the author of *Sarasota School of Architecture, 1941–1966*) that "young apprentices were assigned to guard the [office's] pre-Columbian artifacts, mop floors and fight off rival architects and their apprentices. They would guard the wastebaskets from Paul Rudolph, Bert Brosmith, William Morgan, Jack West, and Tim Seibert. You could tell the level of creative genius/lengths [these other architects] would go to get information: check the toilet/urinal traps…[and also] talk to the wives [of Lundy employees, who would sometimes] take sketches home to dispose. [Apprentices would] also stand guard at the printing shop to see no extra copies were made that would fall into 'enemy hands.' Or [give them a] glimpse!"

16. Victor A. Lundy, "Wood in the Big Perspective of Architecture," in *Design and Aesthetics in Wood*, edited by Eric A. Anderson and George F. Earle (Syracuse, NY: SUNY College of Environmental Science and Forestry, 1972), 104–7. Lundy was one of sixteen invited speakers at this conference, held November 7–9, 1967, at SUNY Syracuse, including such architectural notables as Reyner Banham, Carl Koch, Charles Moore, A. Quincy Jones, and Buckminster Fuller.

17. From north to south, the barrier islands of Sarasota County are Longboat Key, Lido Key, Siesta Key, Casey Key, and Manasota Key. All of Lido Key and the north tip of Siesta Key are in the jurisdiction of the City of Sarasota.

18. In 1969 Field sold the complex to a Buffalo orthodontist, Dr. M. J. "Murf" Klauber, who further developed the facility into a tennis resort comprising 208 one- and two-bedroom villa-suites, 21 tennis courts, 2 waterfront restaurants, and a meeting space for up to 200 people. Three of Field's original cottages were retained, restored, and marketed as nostalgic 1950s vacation experiences. Members

of the club were allowed to occupy their unit for thirty days a year, but had to release it for rental to guests for the remainder of the year, similar to a time-share. At the time of writing (June 2017), Klauber's development, including Lundy's Clubhouse, is slated to be demolished.

19. The businessmen King and Smith eventually developed most of South Sarasota throughout the 1950s and 1960s: South Gate subdivision (starting in 1955), Gulf Gate subdivision (starting in 1957), and Centergate subdivision (starting in 1959). In a full-page *Sarasota Herald-Tribune* advertisement on May 20, 1956, King and Smith declared, "Our faith in Sarasota is boundless. We believe that this city…this entire area…is destined to become one of Florida's great centers of population. More and more people each year 'discover' the West Coast and Sarasota with the great gifts bestowed on her by nature."

20. A South Gate Post Office was also located in this building. Today, the entire building is used by the Post Office—a possible reason for some people's confusion over the architect for the main Sarasota US Post Office on Ringling Boulevard. (See note 32 below.)

21. When preparing for a 1960 meeting with Walter McQuade from *Architectural Forum*, Lundy made notes in his brain book to "show McQuade full color photos of Galloway's, St. Paul's, Frontenac, St. Andrew's [and] B&W's of Galloway's furniture (just in case) + extra photos of Unitarian Church." Within this list—between Frontenac and St. Andrew's—is a note by Lundy indicating his opinion of the Joe Barth project: "(Barth! No!)," perhaps explaining the dearth of period photographs of this building. Regardless, the structure is a staple of downtown Sarasota midcentury architecture and was astutely renovated in 2012 by Murray Homes, which uses it as headquarters.

22. This cylindrical garage has led to (incorrect) rumors that it contains a giant lazy Susan onto which the car drives and gets rotated so that it never needs to back out.

23. "AIA Award of Merit: Warm Mineral Springs Inn," *Florida Architect*, August 1958, 15.

24. Despite its commercial success, Galloway's Furniture Showroom was unfortunately short-lived, closing in the early 1960s. In 1965 the illustrator Ben Stahl (whose house was the reason Lundy came to Sarasota) covered the glass walls with curtains on the interior and used the building to exhibit his famous 1954 "14 Stations of the Cross" paintings. See www.freelaunch.com/museum/history.html (accessed June 14, 2017). In 1977 Sarasota

Optical Center purchased the building and used it without changing the layout. However, in 1986 Visionworks purchased Sarasota Optical Center and went about closing up the glass walls with blockwork, chopping the circular roof into an octagon, and building many interior partitions to create exam rooms, offices, etc., to make the building completely unrecognizable from Lundy's original project. In 2014 the Sarasota Museum of Art (SMOA), a division of the Ringling College of Art + Design, purchased the building because it is adjacent to the museum's main building, the 1926 Collegiate-Gothic-style Sarasota High School, which they are renovating. SMOA intends to renovate Lundy's building at some point, but it is unclear when and to what extent because of the damage suffered from Visionworks in 1987.

25. In reality, the mantelpiece stops at the glass, and another piece starts on the other side. However, the effect is that the mantelpiece passes through the glass.

26. "Two Hospitable Houses Planned for Breezes and Views," *Architectural Record*, August 1960, 174.

27. Lundy's first office was in Guilford, Connecticut, but he soon moved it to New York City—first at 6 E. 65th Street and then 22 E. 67th Street.

28. Florida projects completed by Blackner during this time include St. Paul Lutheran Church, Melbourne (1960); the Bay Hill Country Club, Orlando (1961); Lutheran Church of the Holy Comforter, Treasure Island (1962); and St. Mark Lutheran Church, Orlando (1963).

29. Brains book with the spine listing "1960: Galloway House, Tampa, Florida," Container A263, Victor Lundy Archives, Library of Congress.

30. Brains book with the spine listing "1959–1960: Parsonage & First Unitarian Church (Westport, CT), Hillspoint Elementary School (Westport, CT), Tamiami Building, Ballet Building," Container A263, Victor Lundy Archives, Library of Congress.

31. The Sarasota Mobile Home Park was adjacent to the Payne Park baseball stadium just south of downtown Sarasota. It is interesting to think that this design could have been built instead of the nondescript "Payne Park Auditorium" that was constructed in 1962, presumably after Lundy's proposal was rejected (possibly for cost reasons).

32. In the same way that many people incorrectly attribute well-designed buildings in the United States to Frank Lloyd Wright because they are so good that they *must* be by such a master, there are buildings in Sarasota that are misattributed to Lundy because of their perceived expressiveness. This is, of course, a compliment to Lundy, showing that he "cornered the market" on expressive modern architecture in Sarasota. Two such examples are the Sarasota Post Office (Robert Shaw, 1964) and the Donald-Roberts Company Furniture Showroom, 3201 S. Tamiami Trail, currently the Sarasota Physicians Surgical Center (Carl Vollmer, 1957). The eyebrow canopies on the front facade of the former and the hyperbolic cantilevers of the latter have made some people conclude that they were Lundy projects. Conversely, the author can recount visiting Warm Mineral Springs Motel with *Sarasota Herald-Tribune* Real Estate Editor Harold Bubil in 2013, where the manager behind the check-in desk proudly proclaimed to our tour group that the building's architect was Frank Lloyd Wright, despite the existence of a framed copy of the *Florida Architect* article of the building hanging on the wall. Thankfully, the motel's website, www.warmmineralspring smotel.com (accessed May 29, 2017), correctly identifies Lundy as the architect.

33. "New Ideas of Victor A. Lundy," *Architectural Record*, February 1962, 105.

Sacred Spaces

1. Victor Lundy, Interview by Christopher Domin, April 13–14, 2017.

2. Topics developed in the section were first presented in the Ballroom Marfa catalog for "The Art and Architecture of Anstis and Victor Lundy" exhibition, March 25–June 30, 2006.

3. Victor Lundy, "Art Alone, Untiring, Stays to Us," *Journal of the American Institute of Architects* 31, no. 5 (1959): 18.

4. See also Pietro Belluschi, Zion Lutheran Church in Portland, Oregon (1950), and Lloyd Wright's Wayfarers Chapel in Rancho Palos Verdes, California (1951).

5. "New Ideas of Victor Lundy," *Architectural Record* 131 (February 1962): 105.

6. Victor Lundy, Interview by Christopher Domin, March 1, 2006.

7. "Building Types Study 259," *Architectural Record* 123 (June 1958): 176.

8. Ibid.

9. "Victor Lundy et L'Evolution de la Tradition Architecturale Américaine," *Architecture: Formes et Fonctions*, Lausanne, 26–27 (1964–64).

10. "Address to A.I.A. Wisconsin," April 30,
1964. "Victor Lundy et L'Evolution de la Tradition Architecturale Américaine," *Architecture: Formes et Fonctions*, Lausanne, 26–27 (1964–64).

11. *Fiftieth Anniversary Service Transcript*, First Unitarian Church Westport Archive, Westport, CT.

12. *Explanation of the Building Pamphlet*, First Unitarian Church Westport archive.

13. During the design process for Westport, Lundy traveled to South America and delivered a lecture titled "On What Is Art and Beauty" in Buenos Aires, Argentina. One can imagine that he was influenced by his work with the congregation in Westport: "Architecture is the one art—unlike all others—where all people participate in the actuality—they move through it—they live in it, love and work and play in it—and the great work of art is architecture soon shows itself a non-precious thing."

14. In 1960 the Lundy office had a large number of church projects in various stages of development, including St. Paul Lutheran, Melbourne, FL; St. Andrew Presbyterian, Dunedin, FL; Gloria Dei, Anna Maria Island, FL; Lutheran Church of the Holy Comforter, Treasure Island, FL; First Unitarian Church and Parsonage, Westport, CT; and Westminster Unitarian Church, East Greenwich, RI.

15. Victor Lundy, Interview by Christopher Domin, April 13–14 2017.

16. "The New Church of the Resurrection," *East Harlem Protestant Parish Newsletter*, October 1961, unsigned.

17. Paul Goldberger, *The City Observed: New York* (New York: Random House, 1979), 305.

18. AIA Honor Awards, Award of Merit, July 1966. "The 1966 Honor Awards," *AIA Journal*, 46, no. 1 (1966): 42–43.

19. David W. Dunlap, "A Church Takes a New Form, and Blends into the Cityscape," *New York Times*, October 29, 2008.

20. Goldberger, *City Observed*, 305.

21. "New Ideas of Victor A. Lundy," *Architectural Record* 131 (February 1962): 119.

22. Freeman W. Meyer, *Hartford Unitarianism, 1844–1994* (Hartford, CT: Unitarian Society of Hartford, 1994), 63.

23. Topics developed in the section were first presented at Queens' College Cambridge for the Construction History Society, in 2014.

24. "Church under a Great Tent," *Architectural Forum*, 133, no. 1 (1970): 79.

25. Hannskarl Bandel, a structural engineer and later partner with Severud in his New York–based consultancy, pioneered solutions

to the unique engineering problems associated with suspended roof design, including Hartford Unitarian and St. Paul's Lutheran in Sarasota.
26. "Church under a Great Tent," 79.

United States Tax Court Building

1. Victor A. Lundy, Memorandum, Victor A. Lundy Archive, Library of Congress.
2. US General Services Administration, *Growth, Efficiency, and Modernism: GSA Buildings of the 1950s, 60s, and 70s* (U.S. General Services Administration; Washington, DC: 2005), 29, 38.
3. Antoinette J. Lee, *Architects to the Nation: The Rise and Fall of the Supervising Architect's Office* (New York: Oxford University Press, 2000), 39–41.
4. US General Services Administration, *Growth, Efficiency, and Modernism*, 10–11.
5. Ibid., 6, 38.
6. Ibid., 37.
7. Ad Hoc Committee on Federal Office Space, "Guiding Principles for Federal Architecture," in *Report to the President by the Ad Hoc Committee on Federal Office Space* (Washington, DC: U.S. Government Printing Office, June 1, 1962).
8. Quinn Evans/Architects and Robinson and Associates, *Historic Structures Report: United States Tax Court Building* (Washington, DC: 1996), 5–7.
9. Lundy, Memorandum.
10. Quinn Evans/Architects and Robinson and Associates, *Historic Structures Report*, 9–13.
11. Lundy, Memorandum.
12. Quinn Evans/Architects and Robinson and Associates, *Historic Structures Report*, 8–9.
13. Ibid., 9–10.
14. Ibid., 7.
15. Ibid., 10.
16. Ada Louise Huxtable, "Architecture: Full Speed Forward," *New York Times*, October 1, 1967.
17. "Justice on a Pedestal," *Architectural Forum*, September 1967, 76.
18. Quinn Evans / Architects and Robinson and Associates, *Historic Structures Report*, 12.
19. Ibid., 10.
20. Ibid.
21. Ibid., 13.
22. Quoted in Stanley Abercrombie, "Monumental Suspense," *Progressive Architecture*, July 1976, 55.
23. Lundy, Memorandum.
24. Abercrombie, "Monumental Suspense," 58.
25. National Register of Historic Places, United States Tax Court Building, Washington, DC, National Register No. 08000821, 2008.
26. US General Services Administration, *Victor Lundy: Sculptor of Space*, 2014. www.youtube.com/watch?v=s6umLipF7-E.

United States Embassy, Sri Lanka

1. See www.gsa.gov/real-estate/design-construction/design-excellence/design-excellence-program/guiding-principles-for-federal-architecture.
2. Lundy had a rushed meeting with Mr. Nisonger, Mr. Booker, Thomas Pope, and Mr. Del Favro prior to departing for the first site visit in Colombo.
3. Victor Lundy, note dated January 16, 1961, in brains book, Container A263, Victor Lundy Archives, Library of Congress.
4. Ibid.
5. Ibid.
6. Ibid.
7. A few of Lundy's travel sketches from his first trip to Ceylon are documented in "Journey to the East," *Progressive Architecture* 45 (December 1964): 134–45.
8. Lundy, note dated January 16, 1961.
9. Ibid.
10. Victor Lundy, note dated February 2, 1961, in brains book, Container A263, Victor Lundy Archives, Library of Congress.
11. The embassy building program was updated again after December 1, 1978.
12. Note from phone conversation dated November 29, 1976, in brains book, Container A269, Victor Lundy Archives, Library of Congress.
13. The formal presentation of the new chancery to the ambassador and staff took place on August 8, 1978, at 2 p.m. in the office of Ambassador Wriggins. Attendees included Ambassador Wriggins, DCM Herbert Levin, Ralph Hartwell, Charles Nichols, Richard Von Glatz, A. Agnew, Thomas Arndt, Alan Dahl, Tony Garcia, Victor Lundy, Rex Hellman, Walter Notheis, and other staff members. Multiple additional formal and informal meetings took place on that same trip to Colombo.
14. Lundy, note dated January 16, 1961.
15. The then recently built German embassy had imported most of its building materials.
16. Lundy worked hard to keep the sand-colored stone in the project even though a less expensive gray stone from Bangalore was being pushed. Lundy had to strongly remind FBO that as the architect, he was in charge of aesthetics.
17. Lundy's hand-drawn details are dated August 10, 1979. The stone shop drawings are dated March 6, 1980 (Victor Lundy Archives, Library of Congress).
18. Victor Lundy, interview by author, Bellaire, TX, July 18, 2016.
19. Lundy, note dated January 16, 1961.
20. Victor Lundy to Anstis Lundy, envelope tucked into a brains book, dated April 20, 1984–May 21, 1984, Victor Lundy Archives, Library of Congress.
21. Lundy, interview by author.
22. See overseasbuildings.state.gov/about/message/.

Houston Projects

1. Lundy's tenure at the University of Houston is not referenced in *Open Plan: The History of the College of Architecture, University of Houston, 1945–1995* (Houston: Atrium, 1995). Nor does his name appear in *HKS: Selected and Current Works* (Mulgrave: Images Publishing Group, 2001), documenting the work of the architecture firm founded by Harwood K. Smith in 1939. See also John Howey, *The Sarasota School of Architecture, 1941–1966* (Cambridge, MA: MIT Press, 1995), 143–54, 174–76.
2. *Counting: Essays in Honor of Anderson Todd*, ed. Ron Witte (Houston: Rice School of Architecture, 2011) and John Zemanek, *Being, Becoming: An Acorn is to Become an Oak* (Houston: privately printed, 2016).

Sculpting Space

1. Victor Lundy, note dated February 20, 1961, in brains book, Container A263, Victor Lundy Archives, Library of Congress. In his Diary of Trip to Colombo, Lundy notes the specifications for the plaster mix and black polished floors of Padmanabhapuram Palace.
2. An image of the Bee Ridge church was even featured in an advertisement for Southern Pine titled *Behold, the Renaissance of Wood*.
3. Lundy became well known for his wood structures. In 1959 he received a note about a shipment of aged black cypress; even suppliers were learning of his love for authentic materials.
4. Victor Lundy, AIA award entry text, Library of Congress.
5. Victor Lundy, "A New Wave of Wood," *Architectural Forum* 116 (June 1962): 126.
6. Victor Lundy, interview by author, Bellaire, TX, April 18, 2017.
7. Lundy, "New Wave of Wood," 123–27.
8. Preliminary design drawings are dated May

15, 1964. Shop drawings were produced in October 1964. The permit set was completed on November 25, 1964.

9. A note on the section drawings states that the builder is to "form to gradual curve under supervision of architect."

10. O.G., "Magic Architecture for the Singer Sewing Center," *Interiors* 125 (August 1965): 89.

11. Incor 24-hour Portland cement.

12. "From Uxmal to IBM," *Time* magazine, July 2, 1965, 39.

13. On November 20, 1963, Lundy attended the "Design and Construction Innovation of Wood and Related Structures" conference at Columbia University in New York City. On April 17, 1965, Lundy attended a conference on structure in architecture, held in Washington, DC.

14. Richard Ingersoll, *World Architecture, 1800–2000: A Critical Mosaic* (New York: Springer-VerlagWien, 2000), 1: xliv.

15. Lundy, AIA award entry text.

16. Victor Lundy to Mr. Edward Gardner, director of the office of special projects of the US Atomic Energy Commission, April 29, 1960.

17. Selection considerations mentioned in Lundy's report include portability, high structural efficiency, ease and rapidity of erection and striking, minimum weight, minimum bulk, ease of repeated assembly, minimum trained personnel required for erection and maintenance, minimum site preparation, relatively low cost; dual envelope structure is good for light, heat, sound control. A March 31, 1960, proposal from Birdair stated that shipment would take place sixteen weeks after receipt of order.

18. Mimi Zeiger, *Victor Victorious*, October 2008, mimizeiger.com/VICTOR-VICTORIOUS/.

19. The walls weighed only six tons.

20. David Allison, "A Great Balloon for Peaceful Atoms," *Architectural Forum*, November 1960, 142–44.

21. The exhibit was in Rio de Janeiro in March 1961 and Lima, Peru, in October 1961.

22. Brass Rail had the sole license to provide Carlsberg beer at the fair.

23. Lundy, interview, Bellaire, TX, July 18, 2016.

24. The "International Colloquium in Pneumatic Structures" was held at the University of Stuttgart, West Germany. The conference was hosted and the proceedings were published by the International Association for Shell Structures.

25. Victor Lundy, interview by author, Bellaire, TX, April 18, 2017.

26. The firm has changed names and is now Severud-Perrone-Fischer-Sturm-Conlin-Bandel Consulting Engineers.

27. Victor Lundy, interview by the author, February 29, 2016.

28. Nicolas Lundy, note to author, May 17, 2017.

Chronology

Victor Alfred Lundy

1923
February 1, born in New York City

1933
Family moved to St. Petersburg, Russia, for one year, returned via Brussels

1934
Family returned to US

1939
Graduated from DeWitt High School and received scholarship to attend New York University

1939–1940
New York University, University College of Arts and Future Science

1940–1943
New York University, School of Architecture and Allied Arts

1943–1945
Enlisted in Army Specialized Training Program; served as US Army Combat Infantryman; Squad Leader, with the 26th Infantry Division, General Patton's Third Army in Europe, Northern France, and Rhineland Campaigns

1944
November 12, wounded in action, Rodalbe, France

1945
Bachelor of Architecture, Harvard University

1947
Married Shirley Corwin, divorced in 1959. Had two children: Christopher Mark, Jennifer Alison

1948
Master of Architecture, Harvard University

1948–1950
Rotch Travelling Scholarship, Travelling Fellow

1950
November 5, passed the architecture licensing exam in New York

1951
Moved to Sarasota with wife, Shirley

1951–1960
Private practice, Sarasota, Florida

1956
Award of Merit, Southeast Region AIA: The Venice-Nokomis Presbyterian Church, Outdoor Garden Sanctuary, Venice, Florida

Award of Merit, Southeast Region AIA: Florida's Silver Spring Tourist Center, Silver Springs, Florida

1957
Exhibition: Florida's Silver Springs Tourist Center, Silver Springs, Florida

Exhibition: The São Paulo International Biennial Exhibition of Architecture at the Museu De Arte Moderna in São Paulo, Brazil. One of thirteen US Architects in a travelling exhibition of architecture throughout South America

Award of Merit, Southeast Region AIA: The Bee Ridge Presbyterian Church, Sarasota, Florida

Exhibition: Work displayed with that of the American architects in "America Builds," at the Berlin International Architectural Exposition

Visiting Critic, Harvard University Graduate School of Design. Worked with students in the final year of their bachelor's degrees

1958
Visiting Lecturer, University of California, Berkeley

Speaker at the 1958 Convention of the California Council, Monterey, California

Award of Merit, Southeast Region AIA: Warm Springs Inn, Venice, Florida

Exhibition: Architectural work selected by the American Institute of Architects and the State Department for inclusion in the Exhibition of the United States Section at the Fifth Congress of the Union International des Architectes, held in Moscow

Progressive Architecture Award: Warm Mineral Springs Inn, Venice, Florida

Jury: Felix Candela, Arthur Davis, Henry Kamphoefner, Carl Koch, I. M. Pei

Architectural Record Award of Excellence: For house design presented in *Record Houses of 1958*

Award of Merit, Southeast Region AIA, 1958: Florida's Silver Springs Tourist Center, Silver Springs, Florida

1959
Award of Merit, Southeast Region AIA: Galloway Furniture Showroom, Sarasota, Florida

First Honor Award, American Institute of Architects, for outstanding contribution to Homes of Better Living, in cooperation with *House and Home* and *McCall's* magazines

Speaker at the American Institute of Architecture, Fourth Annual Student Forum, the Octagon, Washington, DC

1959
Creative Assessment in Berkeley, California, April 24–26, 1959, with Barnes, Born, Emons, Johnson, Kirk, Rapson, Saarinen, Warnecke, and Ain

1960
Established office in New York City

Married Anstis Manton Burwell, September 19, 1960, in New York City, had one child: Nicholas Burwell

Silver Medal, Architectural League, New York

Progressive Architecture Design Award: The First Unitarian Church of Fairfield County, Westport, Connecticut

Award of Merit, Southeast Region AIA: St. Paul's Lutheran Church, Sarasota, Florida

National Gold Medal, Exhibition of the Building Arts, Architectural League of New York: The First Unitarian Church of Fairfield County, Westport, Connecticut

Gold Medal Award, Buenos Aires Sesquicentennial International Exhibition: For the Air-Supported Exhibition and the Exhibit for the US Atomic Energy Commission

1962
National Gold Medal, Exhibition of the Building Arts, Architectural League of New York: Galloway Furniture Showroom, Sarasota, Florida

1963
Exhibition: The American Institute of Architects, Hillspoint Elementary School, Westport, Connecticut. Exhibited in the School Building Architectural Exhibit at the Octagon, Washington, DC

Exhibit of architecture at Avery Hall, and visiting lecturer, Columbia University, School of Architecture, New York

Visiting lecturer, Yale University, School of Architecture

1964
First Honor Award, New York Chapter AIA: The First Unitarian Church of Fairfield County, Westport, Connecticut

Exhibition: The American Federation of Arts, Hillspoint Elementary School, Westport, Connecticut

1965
Federal Grant, Department of State, Cultural Exchange Program. Served as a US Specialist-Architect in the Soviet Union in connection with the U.S.I.A. Exhibit "architecture USA" and travelled to the Soviet Union, India, Egypt, and Greece. Served as one of five American architects, including Louis Kahn, Robert Venturi, Paul Rudolf, and Charles Eames

Silver Medal Award, Architectural League of New York, in the 1965 Gold Medal Exhibition of the Building Arts for the Travelling Exhibition Building and Exhibit for the US Atomic Energy Commission in South America, Europe, and the Near East

First Honor Award, New England Region AIA: The First Unitarian Congregational Church of Hartford, Connecticut

Fellow in American Institute of Architects

1966
Award of Merit, American Institute of Architects: Church of the Resurrection, East Harlem, New York City

1967
Speaker at the International Colloquium in Pneumatic Structures. Invited participant on air-supported and cable tension structures at an international conference at the University of Stuttgart, West Germany, International Association for Shell Structures

Visiting lecturer, Montana State University

1970
Work represented in the Exhibit of US Architecture in the US Pavilion at EXPO '70, in Osaka, Japan

Award of Excellence for Interior Design by *Architectural Record*, Record Interior of 1970, Singer Showroom

1972
GSA Honor Award: United States Tax Court, Washington, DC. This project was selected from sixty-five projects to receive the Honor Award in the General Services Administration's first Biennial Design Award Program

1975
Visiting professor and lecturer, School of Architecture and Environmental Design, California Polytechnic State University

Visiting lecturer, College of Architecture, University of New Mexico

Speaker, American Institute of Architects, Santa Barbara Chapter, Monterey Chapter, California

1976–1984
Adjunct professor of architecture, College of Architecture, University of Houston

1979–
Victor A. Lundy & Associates, Inc., Houston, Texas

1982–1987
Design Principal, Taylor/Lundy Partnership with HKS, Houston, Texas

1987–1998
Vice President and Design Principal, HKS Inc., Dallas, Texas. Commuted between Houston and Dallas

1988
United States Presidential Design Awards, 1988 Federal Design Achievement Award: US Embassy Colombo, Sri Lanka (Ceylon). This project was selected from more than five hundred submissions and received the Federal Design Achievement, the National Endowment for the Arts' highest honor in design

2006
Beyond The Harvard Box: The Early Works of Edward L. Barnes, Ulrich Franzen, John Johansen, Victor Lundy, I. M. Pei, and Paul Rudolph, October 5–November 15, 2006, Harvard University Main Gallery, curated by Michael Meredith

2008
US Tax Court Building listed in the National Register of Historic Places

2009
Lundy and the Library of Congress finalize agreement to transfer architectural archive from Texas to Washington, DC

November 20, 2009, Anstis Lundy died

2014
Venice Biennale, work represented in US Pavilion in Venice, Italy

GSA produced the film *Sculptor of Space*

2016
Sarasota Architecture Foundation Lifetime Achievement Award

Project List

While in active practice Lundy was a registered architect in the states of: New York, California, Colorado, District of Columbia, Florida, Georgia, New Jersey, New Mexico, North Carolina, Rhode Island, and Texas. Currently he is an emeritus architect in the state of Texas.

Knight + Lundy, New York City
Stahl House
Year started: 1951
Year completed: 1954
Sarasota, Florida

Victor Lundy Architect, Sarasota, Florida
"Drive-in Church"
Client: The Venice-Nokomis Presbyterian Church
Year started: 1953
Year completed: 1954
Demolished: 1965
Venice, Florida

Berk Residence
Year started: 1954
Year completed: 1954
Sarasota, Florida

Pure Ice Company
Year started: 1954
Not completed
Nokomis, Florida

Sarasota County Chamber of Commerce Building
Client: Sarasota County
Year started: 1955
Year completed: 1956
Sarasota, Florida

The Venice-Nokomis Presbyterian Church Fellowship Hall and Sunday School Building
Client: The Venice-Nokomis Presbyterian Church
Year started: 1955
Year completed: 1956
Surrounded by another structure in 1965, the interior is intact
Venice, Florida

Bee Ridge Presbyterian Church
Year started: 1956
Year completed: 1956
Exterior addition and renovation in 1970 by architect James Padgett
Sarasota, Florida

King & Smith Office Building
Client: Rolland King and Frank Smith
Year started: 1956
Year completed: 1956
Sarasota, Florida

South Gate Community Center
Year started: 1956
Year completed: 1956
Sarasota, Florida

"Inter-American Center" (Interama)
Year started: 1956
Not completed
Miami, Florida

Colony Beach Club
Year started: 1956
Year completed: 1957
Longboat Key, Florida

Dudley Residence
Year started: 1956
Year completed: 1957
Siesta Key, Sarasota, Florida

Alta Vista Elementary School, Addition
Client: Sarasota County Public Schools
Year started: 1956
Year completed: 1958
Sarasota, Florida

Eareckson Residence
Year started: 1957
Year completed: 1957
Siesta Key, Sarasota, Florida

Herron House
Year started: 1957
Year completed: 1957
Renovated in 2014 by others
Venice, Florida

Joe Barth Insurance Company Building
Year started: 1957
Year completed: 1957
Sarasota, Florida

Silver Springs Tourist Center
Year started: 1957
Year completed: 1957
Silver Springs, Florida

Elvgren Residence
Year started: 1957
Year completed: 1959
Siesta Key, Florida

"America Builds" International Architectural Exposition
Berlin, Germany
1957

Waldman Office Building
Year started: 1958
Year completed: 1958
Sarasota, Florida

Warm Mineral Springs Motel
Year started: 1957
Year completed: 1958
North Port, Florida

St. Paul's Fellowship Hall
Client: St. Paul's Evangelical Lutheran Church
Year started: 1958
Year completed: 1959
Sarasota, Florida

St. Andrew's Presbyterian Church
Year started: 1959
Year completed: 1960
Dunedin, Florida

St. Paul's Lutheran Church
Year started: 1958
Year completed: 1960
Melbourne, Florida

Galloway's Furniture Showroom
Client: Ralph M. Galloway
Year started: 1959
Year completed: 1959
Sarasota, Florida

The Frontenac Hotel
Year started: 1959
Year completed: 1959
Lido Key, Sarasota, Florida

Parsonage Building
Client: First Unitarian Church of Fairfield
County, Unitarian Universalist Congregation
Year started: 1959
Year completed: 1960
Westport, Connecticut

The Unitarian Church in Westport
Client: First Unitarian Church of Fairfield
County, Unitarian Universalist Congregation
Year started: 1959
Year completed: 1961
Enclosed: 1965
Westport, Connecticut

Church of the Resurrection
Client: East Harlem Protestant Parish
Year started: 1959
Year completed: 1965
New York City, New York

Pine Shores Presbyterian Church
Year started: 1959
Not completed
Sarasota, Florida

Bay Hill Clubhouse
Client: Bay Hill Country Club
Year started: 1960
Year completed: 1960
Orlando, Florida

Church of the Holy Comforter
Year started: 1960
Year completed: 1960
Treasure Island, Florida

Education Building
Client: St. Paul's Lutheran Evangelical Church
Year started: 1960
Year completed: 1960
Sarasota, Florida

Southgate Office Building
Clients: Rolland King and Frank Smith
Year started: 1960
Year completed: 1960
Sarasota, Florida

Galloway Residence
Client: Ralph M. Galloway
Year started: 1960
Not completed
Tampa, Florida

Sarasota Ballet Building
Year started: 1960
Not completed
Sarasota, Florida

Sarasota Mobile Home Park Community Center
Year started: 1960
Not completed
Sarasota, Florida

Gloria Dei Lutheran Church
Year started: 1960
Year completed: 1962
Anna Maria Island, Florida

Victor Lundy Architect, New York City
Hillspoint Elementary School
Year started: 1960
Year completed: 1961
Westport, Connecticut

Atoms for Peace: Traveling Air Supported
Exhibition Building and Exhibition on the
Peaceful Uses of Atomic Energy
Client: US Atomic Energy Commission
Year started: 1960
Year completed: 1962
Buenos Aires, Rio de Janeiro, Lima, Mexico
City, Santiago, Bogota
Rehabilitated and traveled to: Dublin, Ankara,
Tehran, Baghdad, and Tunis

Sierra Blanca Ski Center Complex
Year started: 1961
Year completed: 1961
Ruidoso, New Mexico

I Miller Showroom
Year started: 1961
Year completed: 1962
Demolished: 1991
New York City, New York

United States Embassy
Client: Office of Foreign Building Operations,
US State Department
Year started: 1961
Year completed: 1984
Colombo, Sri Lanka

Memorial to President Franklin D. Roosevelt
Competition Entry
Year started: 1961
Not completed

Hartford Unitarian Meeting House
Client: First Unitarian Congregational Church
Year started: 1962
Year completed: 1964
Hartford, Connecticut

St. Mark's Lutheran Church
Year started: 1962
Year completed: 1964
Demolished
Orlando, Florida

Westminster Unitarian Church
Year started: 1962
Not completed
East Greenwich, Rhode Island

"Space Flowers" for the New York World's
Fair Refreshment Stands
Client: Brass Rail Refreshment Centers
Year started: 1963
Year completed: 1964
Flushing Meadows, New York

IBM Garden State Office Building
Year started: 1964
Year completed: 1964
Demolished
Cranford, New Jersey

Singer Company Showroom
Year started: 1964
Year completed: 1965
Demolished
New York City, New York

Shade and Structures for the terrace of the
National Museum of History and Technology
(National Museum of American History)
Client: Smithsonian Institution
Year started: 1965
Year completed: 1965
Demolished: 1973
Washington, DC

United States Tax Court Building
Client: General Services Administration, Public
Buildings Service
Year started: 1965
Year completed: 1975
Washington, DC

St. Paul's Sanctuary
Client: St. Paul's Lutheran Evangelical Church
Year started: 1966
Year completed: 1969
Sarasota, Florida

Heller Residence
Year started: 1966
Not completed
Long Island, New York

Education Building
Client: St. Bernard's School
Year started: 1967
Year completed: 1969
Gladstone, New Jersey

University Methodist Chapel,
Florida State University
Client: Wesley Foundation
Year started: 1967
Year completed: 1970
Demolished: 2018
Tallahasse, Florida

Harry Lebensfeld Residence
Year started: 1967
Not completed
Long Island, New York

Intermediate School 53
Client: New York City Board of Education
Year started: 1968
Year completed: 1973
Queens, New York

Infirmary at Cortland State University
Client: New York State University
Construction Fund
Year started: 1969
Year completed: 1972
Cortland, New York

Parking Structure
Client: New York State University
Construction Fund
Year started: 1969
Not completed
Cortland, New York

Marina & Hotel Inter-American Cultural &
Trade Center
Client: Merrill-Stevens, Dry Dock Corp
Year started: 1969
Not completed
Miami, Florida

Lundy Studio and House
Year started: 1970
Year completed: 1972
Aspen, Colorado

Clifford Residence
Year started: 1970
Not completed
Aspen, Colorado

Smithsonian Exhibition Space
Year started: 1970
Not completed
Washington, DC

United States Tax Court Plaza
Client: General Services Administration, Public
Buildings Service
Year started: 1972
Year completed: 1976
Washington, DC

Community Services Center of Westchester
County
Client: Urban Development Corporation
Year started: 1972
Not completed
White Plains, New York

Lucaya Condominium Buidling
Year started: 1973
Not completed
Bradenton, Florida

High-Rise Condominium Apartment Building
Client: O.F. Smith Enterprises
Year started: 1973
Year completed: 1974
Bradenton, Florida

Exhibition Hall, Pyramid of the Sun
Client: Interama
Year started: 1974
Not completed
Miami, Florida

Multi-use Skyscraper Church
Client: First United Methodist Church of Miami
Year started: 1975
Not completed
Miami, Florida

Mosbacher Residence
Year started: 1977
Not completed
Houston, Texas

Victor A. Lundy & Associates, Inc.,
Houston, Texas
Marina Del Rey Hotel
Year started: 1983
Not completed
San Diego, California

Anstis Burwell Lundy Studio
Year started: 1984
Year completed: 1985
Bellaire, Texas

Lundy House (addition to studio)
Year started: 1987
Year completed: 1988
Bellaire, Texas

Victor Lundy Studio
Year started: 1997
Year completed: 1998
Houston, Texas

Joan Miller Residence
Year started: 2002
Year completed: 2003
Houston, Texas

Lundy Studio/Residence
Year started: 2002
Year completed: 2004
Marfa, Texas

House in Houston
Year started: 2003
Not completed
Houston, Texas

Taylor/Lundy/HKS, Houston, Texas
Design Principal
One Commerce Green
Year started: 1982
Year completed: 1983
Houston, Texas

One Westchase Center
Client: Vantage Companies
Year started: 1983
Year completed: 1984
Houston, Texas

Walnut Glen Tower
Year started: 1983
Year completed: 1985
Dallas, Texas

Radisson Hotel, Austin Centre
Client: Encore
Year started: 1983
Year completed: 1986
Austin, Texas

One Congress Plaza
Year started: 1983
Year completed: 1987
Austin, Texas

Chernitsky Towers
Year started: 1983
Not completed
Houston, Texas

Minneapolis Tower Project
Year started: 1983
Not completed
Minneapolis, Minnesota

Phillips Petroleum Company Building
Competition
Year started: 1983
Not completed
Bartlesville, Oklahoma

The Landmark at Carlson Center
Client: Encore Development Corporation
Year started: 1985
Not completed
Minneapolis, Minnesota

HKS Inc., Dallas, Texas
Vice President and Design Principal
Mack Center II
Client: Mack Corporation
Year started: 1987
Year completed: 1990
Tampa, Florida

Grand Turk Project
Client: Smithsonian Institution
Year started: 1987
Year completed: 1987
Grand Turk Island

Greyhound Corporate Center
Year started: 1988
Year completed: 1991
Phoenix, Arizona

Barnett Bank High Rise Towers
Year started: 1988
Not completed
Jacksonville, Florida

Sheraton Towers Hotel Complex
Year started: 1989
Not completed
Bangkok, Thailand

"Prometey" Central Research Institute of
Structural Materials
Year started: 1991
Not completed
St. Petersburg, Russia

Dallas/Fort Worth Super Speedway
Year started: 1991
Not completed
North Texas

Magdeberg Project Ecological Center
Year started: 1992
Not completed
Magdeberg, Germany

100 Story Tower Proposal
Year started: 1993
Not completed
Houston, Texas

Debsirin Alumni Association Building
Year started: 1993
Not completed
Bangkok, Thailand

Royal Maneeya Masterplan (RMM)
Client: Tinasakti Bhanubandh, Maneeya
Realty Co., Ltd.
Year started: 1993
Not completed
Bangkok, Thailand

Hyatt Hotel Project
Year started: 1993
Not completed
Budapest, Hungary

Nashville Competition, City Stage, Theaters,
Opera Hall
Year started: 1993
Not completed
Nashville, Tennessee

2500 Room Hotel/Casino Project
Year started: 1994
Not completed
Las Vegas, Nevada

Langsuan Residential/Office/Condo Tower
with Retail
Client: Tinasakti Bhanubandh, Maneeya
Realty Co., Ltd.
Year started: 1994
Not completed
Bangkok, Thailand

Residential/Condo/Hotel Tower
Client: Tinasakti Bhanubandh, Maneeya
Realty Co., Ltd.
Year started: 1995
Not completed
Bangkok, Thailand

Jon I. Hagler Center, Donor Hall Offices
Texas A&M Foundation Headquarters
Client: Texas A&M University
Year started: 1996
Year completed: 1999
College Station, Texas

GTE Operations World Headquarters
Year started: 1988
Year completed: 1991
Irving, TX

GTE Corporate Headquarters Design
Competition
Year started: 1988
Not completed, won the competition
Stamford, CT

Paxson Communication
Year started: 1998
Not completed

Foster Insurance Company
Not completed
Irving, Texas

Lanigan Clear Lake Office Building
Not completed

Nixon Building
Not completed
Sarasota, Florida

Convention & Casino Entertainment Complex
Client: Convention & Casino Entertainment
Complex
Not completed
Las Vegas, Nevada

Houston National Bank
Client: Fred Welling
Not completed
Houston, Texas

NASA/Clear Lake City Project
Client: Christopher Development Company
Not completed

PARSEC I, Clear Lake City
Client: Christopher Development Company
Not completed
Houston, Texas

Office Buildings
Client: Corrigan Properties, Inc.
Not completed

Paragon Center
Not completed
Fort Lauderdale, Florida

Regency Centre
Client: LeBlanc/Marrero/Webb Group
Not completed
Baton Rouge, Louisiana

Royal/Central
Client: Dal-Mac Development Corporation,
Yancey-Camp Companies
Not completed
Dallas, Texas

San Diego Competition
Client: Lincoln Property Company, N.C., Inc.
Not completed
San Diego, California

Two Countryside Place Trinity Center
Client: Jackson-Shaw Company
Not completed
Dallas, Texas

Client: Carlson Properties, Inc., Webb
Knighton Ventures, Doebbler Development
Corp., Encore Development Corp.
Not completed
San Antonio, Texas

Contributors

Joan M. Brierton is a senior preservation specialist with the US General Services Administration (GSA). She is a recognized expert in federal preservation law with a specialized interest in the identification, evaluation, and treatment of federal mid-century modern architecture. Joan authored the Historic Structures Report on Victor Lundy's US Tax Court Building and served as project manager for GSA's documentary film *Victor Lundy: Sculptor of Space.*

Christopher Domin is an architect and educator at the University of Arizona and lectures internationally on the topic of regional modernism and technological innovation. Professor Domin is coauthor of the book *Paul Rudolph: The Florida Houses,* published by Princeton Architectural Press.

Stephen Fox is an architectural historian and a Fellow of the Anchorage Foundation of Texas. He is a lecturer in architecture at Rice University and the University of Houston and the author of the *Houston Architectural Guide, The Country Houses of John F. Staub,* and *Rice University: An Architectural Tour* and has contributed to many other books.

Sarah A. Garner is a historic preservation specialist at the US General Services Administration, where she has overseen the agency's first comprehensive program to photograph the five hundred historic buildings under its stewardship, including the US Tax Court Building. She served as historian on the documentary film *Victor Lundy: Sculptor of Space.*

Donna Kacmar, FAIA, is a professor at the University of Houston where she teaches comprehensive and professional level design studios and directs the Materials Research Collaborative. Her built work has received several awards and has been nationally published. Her first book, *Big Little House*, was published in 2015.

Nader Tehrani is the founding principal of Office dA, the dean of Cooper Union's Irwin S. Chanin School of Architecture, and the former head of the department of architecture at the MIT School of Architecture and Planning. His research has focused on the transformation of the building industry, innovative material applications, and the development of new means and methods of construction. He is the recipient of many awards, including the Cooper-Hewitt national design award in architecture, the American Academy of Arts and Letters Architecture Award, and seventeen Progressive Architecture Awards.

C. Ford Peatross is the founding director of the Center for Architecture, Design and Engineering (ADE) in the Prints and Photographs Division of the Library of Congress. During his forty-year tenure he has substantially redefined and expanded the ADE collections by over three million items, including the archives of Paul Rudolph, Victor Lundy, I. M. Pei, and many other distinguished architects and designers. The National Building Museum presented him with its President's Award for lifetime achievement in December 2014.

Christopher S. Wilson teaches architecture and design history at Ringling College of Art and Design in Sarasota, Florida. Wilson's expertise lies in the histories, theories, and reception of modern architecture since its appearance in the late nineteenth century. His most recent book is *Beyond Anitkabir: The Construction and Maintenance of National Memory* (Ashgate Press, 2013).

Index

Credits

Front Cover
I. Miller Showroom, Grand Hall, New York City, 1962. Photograph by George Cserna. Avery Architectural & Fine Arts Library, Columbia University

Page 2
Galloway's Furniture Showroom, view of second floor, 1959. Photograph by George Cserna. Avery Architectural & Fine Arts Library, Columbia University

Foreword
Figs. 1–2: Photographs by George Cserna. Avery Architectural & Fine Arts Library, Columbia University

Preface
Figs. 1–2: Photographs by George Cserna. Avery Architectural & Fine Arts Library, Columbia University

The Life and Works of Victor Lundy
Fig. 1: Photograph by Victor Lundy. Library of Congress, Prints & Photographs Division, LC-DIG-ds-11063

Figs. 2–5: Courtesy of Victor Lundy / Victor Lundy Collection, Bellaire, Texas

Fig. 6: Watercolor by Victor Lundy. Library of Congress, Prints & Photographs Division, LC-DIG-ppmsca-49819

Fig. 7: Library of Congress, Prints & Photographs Division, LC-DIG-ds-11067

Fig. 8: Photograph by Anstis Burwell Lundy. Courtesy of Victor Lundy / Victor Lundy Collection, Bellaire, Texas

Fig. 9: Photograph by Victor Lundy. Courtesy of Victor Lundy / Victor Lundy Collection, Bellaire, Texas

Fig. 10: Library of Congress, Prints & Photographs Division, LC-DIG-ds-07281

Fig. 11: Photograph by Victor Lundy. Library of Congress, Prints & Photographs Division, LC-DIG-ds- 11062

Fig. 12: Library of Congress, Prints & Photographs Division, LC-DIG-ds-11080

Fig. 13: Photograph courtesy US General Services Administration (GSA)

Artist Architect
Fig. 1: Library of Congress, Prints & Photographs Division, LC-DIG-ppmsca 51563

Figs. 2–3: Courtesy of Victor Lundy / Victor Lundy Collection, Bellaire, Texas

Fig. 4: Library of Congress, Prints & Photographs Division, LC-DIG-ppmsca-24220

Fig. 5: Library of Congress, Prints & Photographs Division, LC-DIG-ds-11079

Fig. 6: Library of Congress, Prints & Photographs Division, LC-DIG-ppmsca 53481

Fig. 7: Library of Congress, Prints & Photographs Division, LC-DIG-ds-11071

Fig. 8: Library of Congress, Prints & Photographs Division, LC-DIG-ds-11070

Fig. 9: Library of Congress, Prints & Photographs Division, LC-DIG-ds-11072

Fig. 10: Library of Congress, Prints & Photographs Division, LC-DIG-ds-11085

Fig. 11: Library of Congress, Prints & Photographs Division, LC-DIG-ppmsca-53490

Fig. 12: Library of Congress, Prints & Photographs Division, LC-DIG-ppmsca 53491

Fig. 13: Library of Congress, Prints & Photographs Division, LC-DIG-ds-10997

Fig. 14: Courtesy of Victor Lundy / Victor Lundy Collection, Bellaire, Texas

Fig. 15: Library of Congress, Prints & Photographs Division, LC-DIG-ppmsca 53484

Fig. 16: Library of Congress, Prints & Photographs Division, LC-DIG-ppmsca 53485

Fig. 17: Library of Congress, Prints & Photographs Division, LC-DIG-ppmsca 53489

Fig. 18: Library of Congress, Prints & Photographs Division, LC-DIG-ppmsca 53488

Fig. 19: Library of Congress, Prints & Photographs Division, LC-DIG-ppmsca 53493

Fig. 20: Library of Congress, Prints & Photographs Division, LC-DIG-ppmsca 53495

Fig. 21: Library of Congress, Prints & Photographs Division, LC-DIG-ppmsca 53494

Fig. 22: Library of Congress, Prints & Photographs Division, LC-DIG-ppmsca-53496

Fig. 23: Library of Congress, Prints & Photographs Division, LC-DIG-ppmsca-53498

Fig. 24: Library of Congress, Prints & Photographs Division, LC-DIG-ppmsca-53497

The Sarasota Years
Fig. 1: Photograph by George Cserna. Avery Architectural & Fine Arts Library, Columbia University

Fig. 2: Photograph by Joseph Janney Steinmetz, courtesy of Harvard Art Museums (Harvard Art Museums/Fogg Museum, Transfer from the Carpenter Center for the Visual Arts, American Professional Photographers Collection)

Fig. 3: Photograph by Florida News Bureau, courtesy of Florida Memory, State Library and Archives of Florida.

Fig. 4: Courtesy of the Sarasota Architectural Foundation

Figs. 5–6: Photograph by George Cserna. Courtesy of Victor Lundy / Victor Lundy Collection, Bellaire, Texas

Fig. 7: Library of Congress, Prints & Photographs Division, LC-DIG-10984

Fig. 8: Library of Congress, Prints & Photographs Division, LC-DIG-10978

Fig. 9: Photograph by George Cserna. Courtesy of Victor Lundy. Library of Congress, Prints & Photographs Division, LC-DIG-11018

Fig. 10–11: Photographs by Brian Sokolowski. Courtesy of the Sarasota Architectural Foundation

Fig. 12: Photograph by George Cserna. Courtesy of Victor Lundy / Victor Lundy Collection, Bellaire, Texas

Fig. 13: Library of Congress, Prints & Photographs Division, LC-DIG-11048

Fig. 14: Photograph by George Cserna. Courtesy of Victor Lundy. Library of Congress, Prints & Photographs Division, LC-DIG-11051

Fig. 15: Photograph by George Cserna. Courtesy of Victor Lundy. Library of Congress, Prints & Photographs Division, LC-DIG-11050

Fig. 16: Library of Congress, Prints & Photographs Division, LC-DIG-ds-10971

Fig. 17: Photograph by George Cserna. Courtesy of Victor Lundy. Library of Congress, Prints & Photographs Division, LC-DIG-ds-11049

Fig. 18: Photograph by Joseph Scherschel. From The LIFE Picture Collection, Getty Images.

Fig. 19: Library of Congress, Prints & Photographs Division, LC-DIG-ds-10943

Fig. 20: Photograph: Joseph Scherschel. From The LIFE Picture Collection, Getty Images

Fig. 21: Library of Congress, Prints & Photographs Division, LC-DIG-ds-10927

Fig. 22: Library of Congress, Prints & Photographs Division, LC-DIG-ds-10928

Figs. 23–28: Photographs by George Cserna. Avery Architectural & Fine Arts Library, Columbia University

Sacred Spaces
Figs. 1: Photograph by Alexandre Georges. Courtesy of Victor Lundy. Library of Congress, Prints & Photographs Division, LC-DIG-ds-11064

Fig. 2: Photograph by Alexandre Georges. Courtesy of Victor Lundy. Library of Congress, Prints & Photographs Division, LC-DIG-ds-11020

Fig. 3: Photograph by Alexandre Georges. Courtesy of Victor Lundy / Victor Lundy Collection, Bellaire, Texas

Fig. 4: Courtesy of Victor Lundy / Victor Lundy Collection, Bellaire, Texas

Fig. 5: Library of Congress, Prints & Photographs Division, LC-DIG-ds-10939

Figs. 6–9: Photographs by George Cserna. Avery Architectural & Fine Arts Library, Columbia University

Fig. 10: Library of Congress, Prints & Photographs Division, LC-DIG-ds-10950

Fig. 11: Photograph by George H. Cardoso. Courtesy of Westport Unitarian Archive and Robert Zuckerman

Fig. 12: Rendering by Victor Lundy. Photograph by Rob Zuckerman. Courtesy of Westport Unitarian Archive

Fig. 13: Library of Congress, Prints & Photographs Division, LC-DIG-ds-11087

Fig. 14: Library of Congress, Prints & Photographs Division, LC-DIG-ds-10941

Figs. 15–17: Photographs by George Cserna. Avery Architectural & Fine Arts Library, Columbia University

Fig. 18: Library of Congress, Prints & Photographs Division, LC-DIG-ds-11015

Fig. 19: Library of Congress, Prints & Photographs Division, LC-DIG-ds-10946

Fig. 20: Library of Congress, Prints & Photographs Division, LC-DIG-ds-10989

Fig. 21: Library of Congress, Prints & Photographs Division, LC-DIG-ds-10986

Fig. 22: Library of Congress, Prints & Photographs Division, LC-DIG-ds-10985

Figs. 23–26: Photographs by George Cserna. Avery Architectural & Fine Arts Library, Columbia University

Fig. 27: Library of Congress, Prints & Photographs Division, LC-DIG-ds-11109

Fig. 28: Library of Congress, Prints & Photographs Division, LC-DIG-ds-11110

Fig. 29: Photograph by George Cserna. Avery Architectural & Fine Arts Library, Columbia University

Fig. 30: Library of Congress, Prints & Photographs Division, LC-DIG-ds-11111

Figs. 31–36: Photographs by George Cserna. Avery Architectural & Fine Arts Library, Columbia University

The United States Tax Court Building
Fig. 1: Photograph by George Cserna. Courtesy of Victor Lundy / Victor Lundy Collection, Bellaire, Texas

Fig. 2: Library of Congress, Prints & Photographs Division, LC-DIG-ds-10935

Fig. 3: Library of Congress, Prints & Photographs Division, LC-DIG-ds-10842

Fig. 4: Library of Congress, Prints & Photographs Division, LC-DIG-ds-10936

Fig. 5: Library of Congress, Prints & Photographs Division, LC-DIG-ds-11089

Fig. 6: Library of Congress, Prints & Photographs Division, LC-DIG-ds-10840

Fig. 7: Library of Congress, Prints & Photographs Division, LC-DIG-ds-10925

Fig. 8: Library of Congress, Prints & Photographs Division, LC-DIG-ds-11095

Fig. 9: Photograph by George Cserna. Courtesy of Victor Lundy / Victor Lundy Collection, Bellaire, Texas

Fig. 10: Library of Congress, Prints & Photographs Division, LC-DIG-ds-10981

Figs. 11–12: Photographs by George Cserna. Courtesy of Victor Lundy / Victor Lundy Collection, Bellaire, Texas

Figs. 13–14: Photograph by Lautman Photography. Courtesy of Victor Lundy and the National Building Museum, Washington, DC

Fig. 15: Photograph by Carol M. Highsmith. Courtesy of US General Services Administration.

United States Embassy in Sri Lanka
Fig. 1: Courtesy of Victor Lundy / Victor Lundy Collection, Bellaire, Texas

Fig. 2: Library of Congress, Prints & Photographs Division, LC-DIG-ds-10938

Fig. 3: Library of Congress, Prints & Photographs Division, LC-DIG-ds-10933

Fig. 4: Library of Congress, Prints & Photographs Division, LC-DIG-ds-10940

Fig. 5: Library of Congress, Prints & Photographs Division, LC-DIG-ds-11098

Fig. 6: Library of Congress, Prints & Photographs Division, LC-DIG-ds-10934

Fig. 7: Courtesy of Victor Lundy / Victor Lundy Collection, Bellaire, Texas

Fig. 8: Courtesy of the National Building Museum

Fig. 9: Library of Congress, Prints & Photographs Division, LC-DIG-ds-11094

Fig. 10: Library of Congress, Prints & Photographs Division, LC-DIG-ds-10995

Fig. 11: Library of Congress, Prints & Photographs Division, LC-DIG-ds-10945

Fig. 12: Library of Congress, Prints & Photographs Division, LC-DIG-ds-10953

Fig. 13: Library of Congress, Prints & Photographs Division, LC-DIG-ds-10996

Figs. 14–15: Photograph by Jon Henning. Courtesy of Jon Henning

Fig. 16: Photograph by Victor Lundy. Courtesy of Victor Lundy / Victor Lundy Collection, Bellaire, Texas

Fig. 17: Photograph by Victor Lundy. Library of Congress, Prints & Photographs Division, LC-DIG-ds-11059

Fig. 18: Photograph by Victor Lundy. Library of Congress, Prints & Photographs Division, LC-DIG-ds-11058

Fig. 19: Photograph by Victor Lundy. Courtesy of Victor Lundy / Victor Lundy Collection, Bellaire, Texas

Work in Houston
Fig. 1: Photograph by Benjamin Hill

Fig. 2: Library of Congress, Prints & Photographs Division, LC-DIG-ds-10975

Fig. 3: Library of Congress, Prints & Photographs Division, LC-DIG-ds-11000

Figs. 4–7: Photographs by Benjamin Hill

Fig. 8: Library of Congress, Prints & Photographs Division, LC-DIG-ds-10932

Fig. 9: Library of Congress, Prints & Photographs Division, LC-DIG-ds-10980

Figs. 10–13: Photographs by Benjamin Hill

Sculpting Space
Figs. 1–2: Photographs by George Cserna. Avery Architectural & Fine Arts Library, Columbia University

Fig. 3: Library of Congress, Prints & Photographs Division, LC-DIG-ds-10841

Fig. 4: Photograph by Victor Lundy. Library of Congress, Prints & Photographs Division, LC-DIG-ds-11010

Figs. 5–8: Photographs by George Cserna. Avery Architectural & Fine Arts Library, Columbia University

Fig. 9: Library of Congress, Prints & Photographs Division, LC-DIG-ds-10937

Fig. 10: Library of Congress, Prints & Photographs Division, LC-DIG-ds-11001

Fig.11: Library of Congress, Prints & Photographs Division, LC-DIG-ds-11003

Figs. 12–14: Photographs by George Cserna. Avery Architectural & Fine Arts Library, Columbia University

Fig. 15: Library of Congress, Prints & Photographs Division, LC-DIG-ds-10998

Figs. 16–23: Photographs by George Cserna. Avery Architectural & Fine Arts Library, Columbia University

Fig. 24: Library of Congress, Prints & Photographs Division, LC-DIG-ds- 11004

Fig. 25: Photograph by George Cserna. Avery Architectural & Fine Arts Library, Columbia University

Fig. 26: Photograph by Victor Lundy. Library of Congress, Prints & Photographs Division, LC-DIG-ds-11149

Fig. 27: Photograph by George Cserna. Courtesy of Victor Lundy. Library of Congress, Prints & Photographs Division, LC-DIG-ds-11014

Figs. 28–29: Photographs by George Cserna. Avery Architectural & Fine Arts Library, Columbia University

Fig. 30: Library of Congress, Prints & Photographs Division, LC-DIG-ds-10949

Fig. 31: Library of Congress, Prints & Photographs Division, LC-DIG-ds-10930

Fig. 32: Library of Congress, Prints & Photographs Division, LC-DIG-ds-10929

Figs. 33–34: Photographs by George Cserna. Avery Architectural & Fine Arts Library, Columbia University

Fig. 35: Library of Congress, Prints & Photographs Division, LC-DIG-ds-11082

Figs. 36–37: Photographs by George Cserna. Avery Architectural & Fine Arts Library, Columbia University

Page 240
Photograph by George Cserna. Avery Architectural & Fine Arts Library, Columbia University